That Makes Two of Us

Lifestyle Mentoring for Women

by Connie Chandler Witt
and Cathi Workman

Group
Loveland, Colorado
www.group.com

Group resources actually work!

This Group resource incorporates our R.E.A.L. approach to ministry. It reinforces a growing friendship with Jesus, encourages long-term learning, and results in life transformation, because it's

Relational
Learner-to-learner interaction enhances learning and builds Christian friendships.

Experiential
What learners experience through discussion and action sticks with them up to 9 times longer than what they simply hear or read.

Applicable
The aim of Christian education is to equip learners to be both hearers and doers of God's Word.

Learner-based
Learners understand and retain more when the learning process takes into consideration how they learn best.

That Makes Two of Us
Lifestyle Mentoring for Women
Copyright © 2009 Connie Witt and Cathi Workman

Visit our website: **www.group.com/women**

Credits
Executive Developer: Amy Nappa
Chief Creative Officer: Joani Schultz
Art Director: Andrea Filer
Copy Editor: Janis Sampson
Print Production Artist: Amber Gomez Balanzar
Cover Designer: Samantha Wranosky
Production Manager: DeAnne Lear

Unless otherwise indicated, all Scripture quotations are taken from the *Holy Bible*, New Living Translation, copyright © 1996, 2004. Used by permission of Tyndale House Publishers, Inc., Carol Stream, Illinois 60188. All rights reserved.

Library of Congress Cataloging-in-Publication Data
Witt, Connie.
  That makes two of us : lifestyle mentoring for women / by Connie Witt and Cathi Workman.
    p. cm.
  ISBN 978-0-7644-3828-8 (pbk. : alk. paper)
1. Church work with women. 2. Mentoring in church work. I. Workman, Cathi. II. Title.
BV4445.W58 2009
259.082--dc22
                       2008033981

10 9 8 7 6 5 4 3 2 1   18 17 16 15 14 13 12 11 10 09
Printed in the United States of America.

To my husband, Lance.

My best friend, my biggest cheerleader, and my greatest fan.

I love you!

Contents

OK…but How?

Foreword

Connie Witt has taken the intimidating and overwhelming and has turned it into practical and fun. I have spent over 40 years in ministry; every time I teach I look for ways to take difficult truths and make them simple to understand. That is why I so appreciate Connie and her approach to life, ministry, and writing. You will love not only this book, but you will be so ready to invest your life into the women God has brought into your life.

My wife, Norma, has spent the last 40 years mentoring young women, and yet I don't think she ever officially called it mentoring. This book validates what I have believed and practiced my whole life. Norma and I have never walked up to someone and asked, "We would like to be your mentor, is that OK?" I am guessing many avoid mentoring because they think that question needs to be asked. Connie is going to show you in this book how to invest your life without being corny, intimidated, or overwhelmed.

That Makes Two Of Us introduces a real, authentic, vulnerable, and intentional way to invest in the lives of young women. The last thing most of us need is another commitment in our already busy day. Connie helps us see our existing schedules as opportunities to invest in relationships.

In my 40 years of marriage and family ministry, I have seen just about every kind of program and idea for helping people. We've boiled it down to formulas, teaching notes, and catch phrases. Yet, still the most powerful way to be used of God is to give your life away to another. Life on life is still the best "non-program" for mentoring.

Cathi Workman takes us into the mind and heart of younger women. Her insight is priceless. Young women today haven't necessarily grown up with good models. Be it family life, spiritual guidance, or basic life skills. Women today aren't looking for perfect examples but for those willing to share their journey. This book equips you to impact another woman by inviting her into your life.

I have been writing books for years, yet I know that my life is the best curriculum I have to offer. I am teaching every day, and the classroom is the world of relationships I have around me. You too have a curriculum. Allow Connie to help you develop and share your story with the friends you already have.

Thank you, Connie and Cathi, for writing this book. So many lives will be changed as a result of it!

Blessings,
Dr. Gary Smalley

Preface

I would never in a million years have considered myself a mentor. And never in *two million years* thought I would be writing a guide for women on mentoring!

I am not well read or an educator, and I don't consider myself brilliant by any stretch of the imagination! I'm just an everyday woman. I struggle with the same things you struggle with. I love the same stuff you love, and I have vices and temptations just like you do! But God wants to use me, and he wants to use you too!

In my early years as a pastor's wife, I sometimes felt inadequate and underqualified in nearly every area of my life. I knew all of the principles of "spiritual health"; I had the "forsake not the assembly" and "fellowship" down pat. But when it came to discipleship or evangelism, my score card dipped drastically! And when it came to "passing on what I know" and investing in the next generation—forget it!

But a few years ago, I realized I didn't have to be at a certain level with certain criteria before God could use me. In fact, if there was a criteria being set, I was setting it, not God. He was ready to use me at any time, but I had to be ready and willing to step out in faith and act when he put opportunities in front of me.

Looking back over my life, I have been involved in discipling and mentoring moments tons of times. I just didn't see what I was doing as "spiritual." I saw my actions as nothing more than being a friend and hanging out with a younger woman, one just a little behind me in the stages of life.

I see things differently now.

My husband calls it "the gift of hang"—seeing the opportunity to spend time with younger women and intentionally watching for the times I can inject a "God moment" or "life lesson" into the mix.

God wants to use you, right now, just as you are. He probably *is* using you to impact other women, you just don't see it.

That's why *That Makes Two of Us* was developed—so that you can see the younger women God places in your life through a different lens, recognize the opportunities he's put in front of you, and act on them.

It's easy, it's fun, it isn't time intensive, and best of all, it's how God designed discipleship and mentoring to be!

If I can do this, believe me, *you* can do this!

Impacting the Next Generation Through Lifestyle Mentoring

"We will not hide these truths from our children; we will tell the next generation about the glorious deeds of the Lord, about his power and his mighty wonders. For he issued his laws to Jacob; he gave his instructions to Israel. He commanded our ancestors to teach them to their children, so the next generation might know them—even the children not yet born—and they in turn will teach their own children."

Psalm 78:4-6

Several years ago God put a 19-year-old woman in my life named Cathi. We met in the music ministry at our church and shared an instant connection. She worked in the same building as my husband at the church, so I started intentionally dropping by her desk whenever I came to visit him. It was during these impromptu chats that our relationship really began. I started e-mailing her, taking her to lunch, and occasionally calling to check on her. Eventually I asked her to go shopping, or I would call her up and ask her to make a quick Costco run with me. We would talk about all sorts of things, from recipes to ministry. I never would have considered our relationship to be a "mentoring" relationship. But it was!

As the two of us grew closer, I realized Cathi was opening up to me about more personal, even deeper things. She had questions about God, spirituality, the future of the church, the Bible, and even just the everyday stuff of life. I was no expert in these areas and never pretended to be. I tried to let my life speak louder than my words, and she seemed all right with and even drawn to that. God showed me I didn't have to be a Bible scholar or great teacher to mentor. I just needed to have the freedom to be me, to be available, and to be willing to share what I already knew.

After a while Cathi started introducing me to her friends, and we would all spend time together. Before long I realized they were all struggling with the same questions and issues and had few people to turn to for answers other than their peers. That's when I realized the need was so huge! They all needed a woman—a little older, a little wiser, and a little further down the road than they were—who was willing to be real and vulnerable with them. They needed someone to walk *with* them through life situations. They needed someone to listen, not remedy or solve their problems. Someone who would first love them but then talk with them, guide them, and point them in the right direction. They needed someone who loves and trusts God but messes up and is willing to talk about it!

I hate the word *mentoring*!

It became crystal clear that mentoring relationships are the way to connect with the next generation of women. I knew that other women like me were just the ones for the job. But I hate the word *mentoring*. It seems to conjure up thoughts of overwhelming responsibility, endless supplies of wisdom, long-term commitments and time-consuming meetings. So how could I tell women about the great need for mentors without scaring them, overwhelming them, or asking them to add another thing to their already jampacked schedules?

It was then that God started planting the seeds of lifestyle mentoring in my heart, and *That Makes Two of Us* was created.

So how is *That Makes Two of Us* different from conventional mentoring programs? Well, it isn't a "program" at all! *That Makes Two of Us* is an informal, yet intentional mentoring model. It is informal in that it is unstructured; there is no curriculum, there is no formula for how to spend your time, or even a time commitment, and there is no third-party matching (unless you want to count God as that third party!). It is a totally organic process.

Totally organic but completely intentional. You will learn to begin cultivating relationships intentionally as you start to view the next generation through a different lens. You will see conversations as opportunities to share what God has taught you through your own personal experiences and through Scripture. The good news? *You do this through relationship, not a program.*

⚡ Walking through life together ⚡

God has shown me through this journey that mentoring is not just about going through a book or sitting down and doing a Bible study together. It's about walking through life together. It's simple, convenient, fun, but most of all, it is God's plan to help spiritual growth happen.

Now, my personal passion is 20-somethings. Why? I believe this is the forgotten age group. They get out of college and are ready to change the world with enthusiasm and ideals larger than life itself. But with their newfound independence comes the harsh realization that they are very alone. No more youth group to attend, no more classes to occupy their time, and no more parents to fund life's costly adventures. In the midst of this exciting, overwhelming, life-shaping period, who can they turn to? Who can help them navigate the twists and turns of adulthood? The answer…*you!*

Throughout this guide I may refer to the young women in the 20-something age bracket, but whomever God puts in your path—whether 25, 35, or even 18—the same principles apply. God wants to use *you* to touch somebody's life. Bottom line: *Mentoring is not a program; it's a lifestyle.* It's developing a friendship with someone one step behind you in the journey of life, spending time with her, recognizing that God has put the two of you together for a purpose, and making a point to interject life lessons and point out God moments as you go through life *together!*

You may be thinking, "Mentoring can't be that simple!" I assure you it is. Cathi and I have developed the following guide to help you understand lifestyle mentoring and the importance of investing in the women of the next generation. We are confident there is a quality mentor within each of you!

So we ask you to accept our invitation to impact the next generation…life-to-life.

You can do this!

Let us show you how!

Why Does the Next Generation Need a Different Kind of Mentoring?

"And no one puts new wine into old wineskins. For the wine would burst the wineskins, and the wine and the skins would both be lost. New wine calls for new wineskins."

Mark 2:22

Aged wine is valuable and even sought after. During Bible times, when wine was stored in containers made of animal skins, new wine was not poured into used wineskins because as the new wine matured, it would expand, causing the already-expanded skins to burst, ruining the wine and the skins. Instead, new wine was put into fresh new skins that let the wine breathe and expand. Eventually the wine would take on its own flavor within its container. It was unique. After the wine reached its full potential, the wineskins hardened. They had served their purpose. The wineskins were no longer usable.

Now is the time for new wineskins. The new wine, in this case, is the amazingly complex generation called "20-somethings," "Gen Y," "bridgers," "mosaics," "echo boomers," and the younger "Gen X" and "Millenials." Whatever the label you give that generation, they are full of life and flavor and are bursting at the seams to contribute to the world.

To allow this new wine to reach its fullest potential, we need to use a new wineskin. The changes that have occurred in American life over the past 20 years are staggering. The methods we used to reach the next generation 25 to 30 years ago or even *10* years ago are not always effective with this new generation. The way to reach them now is through lifestyle mentoring.

How can we impact them? We must first try to understand them.

> "[Echo boomers] are the first to grow up with computers at home, in a 500-channel TV universe. They are multi-taskers with cell phones, music downloads, and Instant Messaging on the Internet. They are totally plugged-in citizens of a worldwide community." [1]
>
> —Steve Kroft, CBS News correspondent

Children of Baby Boomers

This is the generation born between the years 1977 and 1995. These dates vary depending on the source. But this fact stands firm: This generation is the generation of baby-boomer children. It is the largest generation since the boomers themselves, who are 72 million strong. It is the most-studied generation by sociologists, demographers, and marketing consultants since their parents.

So what? Big deal! It *is* a big deal. This generation are our new leaders. They're already moving into the leadership positions of our companies, churches, and country.

In Thom Rainer's book *The Bridger Generation*, Rainer makes a revealing comparison between the boomer and bridger generations.

Two Different Worlds [2]

Boomers	Bridgers
economic prosperity	economic uncertainty
mother's care	day care
"Father Knows Best"	Father isn't home
Ma Bell	Internet
VD	AIDS
monocultural	Multicultural

Source: *American Demographics* and *The Bridger Generation* by Thom Rainer

I'm a part of the boomer generation, and the differences between me and this new generation are astounding! The things that my generation invented, developed, and discovered have become the normal, everyday, commonplace, and routine tools of 20-somethings.

You may not be part of the boomer generation, but it's likely that the woman God puts in your life will have different perspectives than you. To get a view of what these differences are, I'd like to make a few comparisons between the boomer and bridger generations.

⚹ Computers, cordless phones, and cars ⚹

Think about it. My generation invented the computer. The bridger generation doesn't know how to function without one. My generation started out with a telephone connected to the wall, progressed to a cordless, and then to wireless. Bridgers' phone of choice is cellular. Bridgers are always accessible and don't know what it's like to be someplace where they can't call or talk with someone else.

A little perspective. When I, a boomer, was in the second grade, I vividly remember my parent's purchase of a brand-new car. A sweet teal-colored Chevrolet Impala. The really cool thing about it was that it had *seat belts* in it! A first! Not the shoulder-harness kind, of course…that came later. Just the plain, over-your-lap seat belts. I'll never forget this because I was so excited that I told my second grade class at show and tell—two days in a row! I was sure I was the envy of all my peers. In contrast, the oldest member of the 20-something generation has never known life *without* a seat belt. They came out of the womb, into our arms, into a car seat, and *then* home!

And think about this: Since they were babies, they've been put in front of the TV or at least had the TV on. Now there are actually DVDs geared toward babies.

Their classroom settings have gone from individualized learning to team learning. Educators have realized that this next generation learns best in teams. They do projects in teams, they study in teams, they practice in teams, they compete in teams, and they even test in teams. Why does this method of teaching work? Echo boomers aren't necessarily motivated by the thought of being better than everyone else in their class, as their parents were motivated to be. But they don't want to be the weak link. Therefore they are motivated to work hard so their entire team succeeds! Basically the success of the team takes precedence over the success of the individual.

This generation learned to depend on each other from a very young age. They also began to rely less on the adults in their life. Remember, this is the generation who grew up with baby-boomer parents. The boomer generation is the generation where dual-income households became the norm instead of the exception. So when homework needed to be done, the first step was to call a friend. Networks were developed and established. Homework hot lines helped kids with homework questions when no one was around to answer them.

This generation is also called a pampered generation. They've been protected and coddled since they were born. They have never ridden a bike without a helmet and never learned any "roller" activity without the presence of elbow, wrist, and knee pads. We've cheered them on no matter how bad they were at something. To boost their self-esteem, everybody got a trophy at the end of the season, not just those that stood out in the "talent" pool. The generation lived with a grade-on-the-curve mentality, and some educators even adopted the "independent spelling" philosophy, with the mind set that computers will catch misspelled words at spell check. This "good intention" of the boomer generation has caused 20-somethings to expect the same thing in the work force: reward for a less-than-stellar job.

In contrast, we boomers worked our tails off, and the kid that won everything in every sport always got the Most Valuable Player award. The phrases "Get Tough," "Work hard," and "Finish what you start!" were the mantras of our generation.

And safety gear? *We didn't need no stinking safety gear!* We sat in the back of pickups going down the highway at 70 mph and thought that was crazy cool! We felt special when our parents let us sit in their laps and steer the car. Air bags? What's an air bag? Can you even imagine any of those situations happening today? It's amazing we made it through childhood!

Yes, the boomer generation is a unique generation in itself. We were raised by the builder generation who believed in the values of hard work, efficiency, duty to your country, and sacrifice. They lived through the depression, saw our country attacked, and survived World War II. They encouraged us (boomers) to express ourselves from an early age. Therefore we were the key generation to fight for civil rights. The boomers are the most successful, affluent generation in history. We set high standards for ourselves and expect to achieve them. We are project driven and goal oriented. We aim for a mark and have failed if we don't hit it dead on. And during our journey, we had kids and families. Our kids have watched as we prospered and achieved our goals, yet divorce rates have skyrocketed and families have crumbled.

Echo boomers are a product of this environment. They are used to having to deal with multiple families or have watched their friends with multiple families. We, as parents, tended to lavish material possessions on our children to make up for the lack of time spent with them. At the time, we felt like we were giving them all that we didn't have growing up. And on some levels, we were.

Relationally driven

This generation has responded by being independent, yet they are *relationally driven.* They have their own individual ideas and ideals but want to live them out with a group of friends. Even their choice of employment is influenced by their standard of community. Will they play a vital part of the team? Do they get to speak into the process? What is the chemistry with their co-workers? What is the bigger purpose of their work? What kind of global fingerprint is this company leaving?

We taught them to express themselves. We encouraged them to be whatever they wanted to be and do whatever they wanted to do. We encouraged them to think independently. Bottom line: We raised them to be who they are today.

And though this next generation is definitely independent and suspicious of authority figures, there is an underlying need for adult interaction. The kind of adult that will encourage and exhort them.

The church is not exempt from the suspicions of this generation. Surveys taken by the Barna Group are showing alarming statistics regarding how the next generation is disengaging from the church. In fact, one of their reports found "The most potent data regarding disengagement is that a majority of twentysomethings—61% of today's young adults—had been churched at one point during their teen years but they are now spiritually disengaged (i.e., not actively attending church, reading the Bible, or praying)." [3]

So how do we re-engage this generation? How can God use us to help recapture the hearts of this amazing generation?

In an article for *Relevant* magazine, writer Rex Miller puts it like this, "The real goods…come in the form of faces and names—trusted relationships that turn the Word into flesh. And this is the Church's largest need, greatest opportunity and most pressing challenge: to deliver on the promise of transformation by finding and nurturing mentors." [4]

That's where you and I come in. We have the opportunity to impact this generation. We just have to discard the old wineskins that we've had for years and start using the new ones that are more suitable for the next generation. We can do this! I know because I have witnessed it firsthand.

There is plenty of statistical information in this section. But the truth is, sometimes it's better to hear from one who has been there and is experiencing this every day.

Cathi, now a 20-something herself, worked for a year studying her own generation. She did extensive research on the emergent church and the postmodern movement and explored ways that the church could bridge the gap between the generations. The following section is an overview of what she learned about her generation as a whole.

Notes

1. Steve Kroft, "The Echo Boomers," *60 Minutes* (September 4, 2005), www.cbsnews.com/stories.

2. Thom S. Rainer, *The Bridger Generation,* (Nashville, TN: Broadman & Holman Publishers, 1997), 8.

3. "Most Twentysomethings Put Christianity on the Shelf Following Spiritually Active Teen Years," The Barna Update (September 11, 2006), www.barna.org.

4. Rex Miller, "From Marginal to Mentor," Relevant magazine, www.relevantmagazine.com.

Five Things Everyone Should Know About the Next Generation

Whether you find yourself mentoring a teenager, a 20-something, or a 30-something, there's one thing I'm sure you'll find: We all see the world very differently! These differences can act as barriers, or they can open doors to relationships. It's simply a matter of perspective.

For one year I had the incredible opportunity to research people in my generation and younger (those born after 1964). What I discovered explained so much about the postmodern mind-set, the habits and attitudes of the next generation, and the hurdles that the older generations face in reaching them. I truly believe you can benefit from my findings as well. Of course, we're all individuals and will encompass these characteristics on varying levels, but these descriptors will give you a sneak peek into the heart and worldview of the young woman God has (or will!) put in your life.

Every generation leaves a unique stamp on the world. The builders are a generation committed to hard work, family values, and a respect of authority. The boomers made their mark as a "me-driven" society, committed to individual progress and the accumulation of material wealth.

There are various names for generations, and some variation between what years researchers attach to each generation, but broadly speaking, these are recent generations and the names associated with them.

Builders:	Boomers:	Busters:	Echo boomers:	Millennials:
Born 1922-1945	1946-1964	1964-1976	1977-1994	1995-Today

While the next generation (be it X, Y, echo boomers, or millennials) continues to be studied by everyone from marketers to sociologists, one thing has become quite clear: We hate to be labeled, stereotyped, or generalized. With that being said, there *are* a few important things you should know about the next generation as a whole. So while I must beg the forgiveness of my peers for breaking it down in such simple, general, and perhaps controversial terms, here they are:

1. We are independent. We are a generation of latchkey kids, for the most part raising ourselves between the hours of 3 p.m. and 6 p.m. With two working parents and involvement in every after-school activity and sport possible, family meals were often replaced with drive-throughs and TV dinners. Many of us came from broken homes and mixed families, moving from house to house with a different set of rules for each set of parents and very little stability. We learned to take care of ourselves and look out for our own best interests. We built strong, family-like relationships with our friends, confiding our deepest hurts and greatest joys with our peers instead of our parents. Even at church (for those of us who went), we were separated from the adults and had an age-catered experience for each year of our spiritual journey.

So where does this leave us? Quite simply, longing for guidance but resistant to direction. We don't want a mentor; *we want a friend*. Someone who will believe in us, encourage us, and be a sounding board for all of our random thoughts, questions, fears, hopes, and desires. When we're faced with difficult decisions, we will benefit more from your *support* than your *opinion*. When we're looking for advice, we'll ask for it. In the meantime, share your life experiences with us, the good and the bad stuff, the successes and the mistakes. And give us the freedom to make mistakes of our own.

Over the last 8 years, I have faced a fair share of difficult decisions and situations with Connie by my side. Barring the times when I asked for her advice or when she knew I was considering something that went directly against God's Word, she withheld her explicit advice and was content to offer support and encouragement. She would help me talk things out and think things through. She gave me the space I needed to succeed and fail on my own but was always there to help me deal with the consequences of my decisions, good or bad.

As time goes on, the good decisions come more naturally. I may not talk through each one with Connie, but her influence is evident in every choice I make. I feel confident to make these decisions on my own as my relationship with God has grown and matured, much to the credit of Connie's encouragement.

2. We are highly connected. Let's face it: Technology has set a new standard in communication. Cell phones, e-mails, instant messages, and even cheap airfares ensure that we are able to stay connected with anyone we choose at any time we choose. In the past you may have had to wait until your 10- or 20-year reunion to catch up with your high school classmates. But with social networking services like MySpace, Facebook, and personal blogs, you can keep track of everything from your friends' marital status to their beverage preferences with just the click of a button. "Losing touch" is a thing of the past, much like the home-answering machine or handwritten letter.

So where does this leave us? With an expectation of availability. In a culture where *boundaries* is a buzzword, it's important that you don't communicate your boundaries as barriers. While technology affords a primarily surface-level connection, what we really want is access to *you* and the deepest parts of you.

Knowing that you'll be there when we really need you, that you'll answer the phone when we call, that you won't flake out on our coffee date is important. Knowing that when we meet, you will be *present* and willing to open yourself up. Being vulnerable and real with us means even more.

Availability *doesn't* mean abandoning your priorities; it just means fitting us into them. There have been plenty of times when Connie has kicked me out of her house because she's going to bed or spending time with her husband, kids, or other friends (I mean…she does have a life!). But when it matters, she is there. Whether I need a shopping partner, a shoulder to cry on, or a listening ear, she makes time for me. I've never felt like an inconvenience, a chore, or a ministry project. The time she spends with me is time she wants to spend with me, getting to know me and opening herself up so I can know her.

Of course through the many seasons we've shared together, there have been times when her availability has been limited (like when she was planning her kids' weddings) and times when mine has too (through my *many* job and life transitions). But through each of these seasons, we found ways of communicating that we were in each other's thoughts and prayers, even if it was just through a quick e-mail or text message. Making yourself available to the women in your life will communicate that you care.

3. **We are cause conscious.** Perhaps because of the highly connected nature of our society, we are more aware of how our actions, purchases, and values affect others. Causes, such as HIV/AIDS, poverty, environmentalism, animal rights, slave labor, fair trade, and human trafficking, pull at our heartstrings deeply. In order to display our commitment to what is right and just and to give a voice to the voiceless, we are willing to change our purchasing habits, our eating habits, what coffee we drink, and what companies we support. We long to be part of a cause that is bigger than ourselves, and there are plenty of causes to choose from.

So where does this leave us? Primed to champion the cause of Christ. Don't question our idealism. Show curiosity for our passion, and focus on the cause we have in common: God's kingdom! You may not totally understand us boycotting chocolate Easter eggs, [1] our vegetarian diets, or our enthusiasm for recycling, but you do understand the cause of Christ. Rallying this generation around God and reminding us of the ultimate cause and the ultimate Champion for justice and mercy is something we can be excited and passionate about together.

4. We are multitaskers. It's a fast-paced world; who has the time to focus on just one thing at a time? My generation grew up doing homework in front of the television (without compromising the quality of our work), talking on the phone while driving and scanning our iPods, checking e-mails, browsing the Internet, and eating—all while having in-depth conversations with friends.

So where does that leave us? This multitasking generation is the perfect crowd for lifestyle mentoring. We have no problem diving into the deep stuff of life while strolling the mall or sitting at the park with you and your kids. If you'll listen, we'll talk. Going on a last-minute errand? Call us. Spontaneous doesn't scare us; in fact, we welcome it. If you keep us in mind, we will connect.

Some of the most meaningful conversations I've had with Connie have occurred while cruising the aisles of Costco. If she had waited until she had a free moment to connect with me, those conversations may never have happened. When you look at your schedule, don't see it as a mass of appointments keeping you from connecting with us; see it as windows of opportunity to bring us alongside you.

5. We are naturally suspicious. Wait. Before you roll your eyes or wrinkle your nose, let me explain.

Our parents' generation, inspired by the revolutionaries of their day, brought equal rights and an age of freethinking to the sixties and seventies. No longer bound to accept the social norms of the day, they used their freedom to voice their opposition to war, to criticize the government, and to fight for the rights of all Americans. They used their voices to speak out against anything that undermined their understanding of what life and freedom should be, and they passed these ideals on to us, their children. We were taught to question authority, to stand up for what is right, and to never back down if someone threatened to take away our rights or liberties.

Couple this with the skewed versions of "reality" shown on television and the intricate web of lies and highly publicized scandals among our political leaders and pastors alike, and you have the makings of an incredibly suspicious generation.

So where does this leave us? With a need for authenticity. What people say, what they do, and how they act is generally disjointed. We want to trust you; we really do. Just be real with us. Show us that you live what you believe or at least that you're trying. When you make a mistake (with us or anyone else), own up to it. Don't try to play the "perfect" card. That's not what we're looking for. Your flaws, your scars, your past—that's what makes you real to us.

Most importantly, we do not want to be your project. Set the whole mentoring thing aside. Do you like spending time with us? Do you enjoy our company? If it feels forced, we'll notice. We're not looking for flattery or fakeness. In fact, there's nothing that turns us off more. This relationship should feel natural, not like a blind date. Relax and be real; that's the best way for you to earn our trust. And once you have it, it's not hard to keep.

Scared yet? I hope not. My generation is longing to connect with you. We have so many things we want to ask you, so many things we want to share with you, and so many things to learn from you! Just reach out and show us you care.

Notes

1. Nearly 70 percent of chocolate Easter eggs are made from cocoa grown by child slaves on the West African Coast. For more details see www.stopthetraffik.org.

Mentoring...
It's Not What You Think!

"Your job is to speak out on the things that make for solid doctrine. Guide older men into lives of temperance, dignity, and wisdom, into healthy faith, love, and endurance. Guide older women into lives of reverence so they end up as neither gossips nor drunks, but models of goodness. By looking at them, the younger women will know how to love their husbands and children, be virtuous and pure, keep a good house, be good wives. We don't want anyone looking down on God's Message because of their behavior. Also, guide the young men to live disciplined lives. But mostly, show them all this by doing it yourself, incorruptible in your teaching, your words solid and sane. Then anyone who is dead set against us, when he finds nothing weird or misguided, might eventually come around."

Titus 2:1-8, The Message

If you're expecting some amazing reference material or a detailed to-do list of mentoring moments, this is not it. This is a *totally different* way to view mentoring. No books or curriculum needed. It's not a Bible study. It's women passing on life to younger women. The only curriculum you need is your life experiences, what God has taught you through those experiences, and what he is teaching you now!

Think about it: How many Bible studies have you attended in your life? How many church services have you attended? How many retreats? How many times has God spoken to you through a personal time alone with him? How many times have you read Bible stories to your kids? And what about the relationships God is using to teach you about himself, such as with your friends, your family, your kids, a co-worker, a person in trouble? What about the practical things you've learned? What do you know now that you wish you would have known when you were younger, such as concerning money, relationships, or kids? Those are just a few conduits through which God has been teaching you. The point is, *we all know much more than we think we do*, and we all know way more than we are sharing.

⸺ A new lens ⸺

Start viewing your life through a different lens. You must see your life as a mentoring tool, a source of information to share with others. God has taught you through circumstances, both good and bad. He wants to use those times as teaching points so others can see his work in you.

So change your lens in the area of *how* you teach. *Show* others Christ; don't just tell them about him. Show them through your everyday situations and circumstances how to live a Christ-like life. Share with them the things Christ has taught you as you go throughout your day.

I got a call from a friend in Texas a few days ago. We started talking about mentoring (imagine that!). Her comment to me was, "Oh no! I can't mentor. I need a book or something. I can't do that!" I tried to assure her that not only does she not need a book, but especially in the beginning, she definitely *shouldn't* use a book. She's already mentoring the tons of girls that are at her house 24/7. She just doesn't realize it! When they stand in the kitchen with her and make cookies or she teaches them to make a cake from scratch, she's mentoring them. Then during those fun times, a subject will come up, and she'll tell them what God has taught her in her own life through similar circumstances. Or she'll share what the Scriptures say on a subject—that's mentoring! She just hasn't called it that!

You could very well be mentoring someone right now, but you don't see what you're doing as mentoring. I certainly didn't! And I still don't tell anyone that's what I'm doing! But what I *have* realized is that when the opportunity comes along, and I have the chance to invest in someone God puts in my path, I become more intentional. I become more aware of the times I can interject teachable moments or "God moments" into our conversation. I become more focused on the circumstances and the urgency of our time together. I realize that God gives us those moments not to waste them but to use them to glorify him.

We have to start recognizing these moments as significant and be willing to open up and share ourselves with others when God gives us the opportunity!

I never took a class on how to mentor someone or attended a tea about mentoring or even read a book about it. It just started when we hosted and led a high school Bible study at our house for teenagers. We loved having the teenagers hang out at our house, and we tried to make them feel comfortable, welcomed, and loved in our home.

The home I grew up in was always warm and welcoming, and my parents always had time for my friends. I grew up knowing that was how I wanted the home that I would create to be. I think the mentoring just grew out of that open home. Bible study was on Tuesday nights, but I soon found that kids were stopping by on weekends and weekdays after school just to hang out, rummage through my pantry, and mostly for a hug or an encouraging talk.

I had a small group of girls that I led at the Bible study, and it became normal for them to visit me frequently. I loved on these girls for four years. Just because they graduated from high school didn't seem a good reason not to welcome them into my home and my life. Of course they all didn't come all the time, but a few became regulars at the dinner table and on the weekends, watching TV with the family, playing games with my kids, or just "hanging" with me while I cooked dinner or did laundry. I know these don't sound like exciting things that young girls would want to observe, but oddly enough they loved the fact that I would listen while I worked and that they felt like part of a family. Many of them had moms that worked or were not in the picture due to divorce or other issues, so these girls just loved being around a "mom."

My kids loved having them there (especially as my sons grew older and the girls were always cute!), and my daughter would watch us interact. I knew I was planting seeds during her adolescence, when she might not have been as interested in talking with me if she hadn't seen other high school and now college girls do it so freely. It became normal for me to do the weekly grocery shopping with extra teenagers or college kids along. I think they even picked up little lessons as I talked through what I was going to cook or how expensive things were and how you had to make choices in life about little and big things. Everyday events became opportunities for conversations about raising children, finding a Christian man, or how to treat your family members. There were many days we walked through the grocery store or mall, wiping tears as they opened up and shared secrets and stories that would never have come out in a small-group–Bible study setting in front of other people. The intimacy of sharing life together made these moments possible and comfortable for all of us.

Now as these girls enter adulthood, some marrying and starting to consider families of their own, I look back at those moments of life we shared together, just walking through the everyday issues of living in community, raising a family, and serving God; and I am so thankful for the chance to speak into the lives of these girls in ways that were so natural, so easy, and so fun!

Kathleen Hamer
Portola Hills, California

Get Over Yourself... in a Good Way!

"So, since we're out from under the old tyranny, does that mean we can live any old way we want? Since we're free in the freedom of God, can we do anything that comes to mind? Hardly. You know well enough from your own experience that there are some acts of so-called freedom that destroy freedom. Offer yourselves to sin, for instance, and it's your last free act. But offer yourselves to the ways of God and the freedom never quits. All your lives you've let sin tell you what to do. But thank God you've started listening to a new master, one whose commands set you free to live openly in his freedom!"

Romans 6:15-18, The Message

Freedom in Christ. What does that mean? Is that even attainable? I've heard that term my whole life, and it's always seemed a little ominous to me. What is freedom in Christ really?

Not too long ago, my husband, Lance, was consulting with a church in Vail, Colorado. We were on one of our three-week consulting excursions. After Colorado, we were going to West Palm Beach, Florida, so we had everything from bathing suits to parkas packed. We had four large bags that we brought with us from California to Vail, along with two carry-ons each, with computer paraphernalia to boot…literally! So there was baggage everywhere I looked.

The image of Lance carrying all of this baggage down the stairs into our room in the basement and our baggage taking over our surroundings is what started the wheels turning about our *internal* baggage.

It was one of those days when the snow was coming down outside and the fire was blazing. It was about 11 a.m., and I was still in my pajamas (it was a pajama-type day). As I looked around, it became so clear to me. *The biggest reason mentoring is so difficult is because of the baggage we've been carrying and continue to carry with us where ever we go.* Baggage of who we *think* we ought to be versus embracing the journey God's brought us on to make us who we are.

Out of the blue (or the heavens!) came the thought: freedom in Christ. God wants us to be free to be who we are. And with him living in us, we are "free in Christ"! It was crystal clear! The load is so much lighter when we let go of the baggage that we've been dragging around with us for years.

Dictionary.com defines *freedom* as "the right to enjoy all the privileges or special rights of citizenship, membership, etc., in a community or the like."

We have access to the Father. We are members of his family! We have the right to all the privileges he offers. But we limit ourselves in how we use these privileges because of the baggage we're carrying. We all want to walk in freedom, but we keep dragging heavy, cumbersome baggage everywhere we go.

....

"In view of all this, make every effort to respond to God's promises. Supplement your faith with a generous provision of moral excellence, and moral excellence with knowledge, and knowledge with self-control, and self-control with patient endurance, and patient endurance with godliness, and godliness with brotherly affection, and brotherly affection with love for everyone.

The more you grow like this, the more productive and useful you will be in your knowledge of our Lord Jesus Christ."

2 Peter 1:5-8

"I'm not saying that I have this all together, that I have it made. But I am well on my way, reaching out for Christ, who has so wondrously reached out for me. Friends, don't get me wrong: By no means do I count myself an expert in all of this, but I've got my eye on the goal, where God is beckoning us onward—to Jesus. I'm off and running, and I'm not turning back."

Philippians 3:12-14, The Message

Let's face it. We are who we are. God made us that way. Second Peter 1:5-8 says that as long as we are striving to be more like Christ, he wants to and is going to use us. We don't have to have it all together before we start making a difference for God.

God wants to use us, just as we are, right where we are. He wants to use us with our shortcomings and our achievements. It doesn't matter if we're rich or poor, born in the country or in the city, our color or our shape. It doesn't matter what personality, geographic location, or financial status we have. Because he is in us and we are doing all we can to be like him, we have freedom. No judgment. No scrutiny. Just grace!

What does that have to do with mentoring? We are free to be who God made us to be so we can share what he has taught us with others. Those who God puts in your life are not at all who God will put in my life. I won't be able to touch the lives of the people that you will be able to touch. That's why we all have our different journeys, our different backgrounds, and histories. So we can impact those that God puts in our path and share our journey with them.

⚹ Freedom for the future ⚹

A light came on in my head in that Colorado basement, and I realized that God wants to use me no matter where I am in the journey. He wants to use all of me, not just the parts that most closely resemble him. He wants to use the good, the bad, and the ugly parts. He wants to use the parts people see and the parts people haven't seen. He wants to use *all* of those parts to help someone else on *her* journey.

Let's get real honest here. What kind of people do you like being around more: those who are transparent, honest, and a little rough around the edges? or those who have it all together, with perfect families, and who know the answer to any and all questions thrown their way? For me, it's the first kind of person. I like to know that I'm not the only one who doesn't have it all together. I like to know that just because I say "crap!" or my husband and I fight doesn't mean I'm backsliding or "sinful." I'm not saying that the second woman *is* saying that. I'm just saying that sometimes I find myself feeling unworthy, less of a person or even less of a Christian because I *am* struggling with those things.

So let's not compare. Let's just agree to get better. You talk about freedom! This is a great way to look at the future. I don't have to be like someone else. I *shouldn't* be like someone else. I need to be who God made *me* to be! I need to be willing to let him use me with all my rough edges exposed. I need to allow him to smooth those edges. But in the process, be available and willing for him to work or speak through me!

We all want to be better, in every aspect of life. And as we get better, let's choose to take someone along with us to see what that looks like. All of it! To see us as we screw up and as we succeed. To watch us as we continue to move forward knowing we aren't perfect and we don't have it all together; but at least we know it, admit it, embrace it, and will act on it! We're intentionally looking toward Christ to improve our walk with him. That's freedom. Freedom to go forward without fear because he knows our heart. We want to walk closer to him. We want to be more like him…everyday!

⚹ Freedom in the now ⚹

God wants to use us. He wants to use *who* we are today. *What* we are today. *How* we are today.

What does that mean? It means he wants to use our experiences, our successes, our failures, our loves, our hurts, our lives!

He wants you to share your story. Sharing your experience and your story with younger women is the key to relationship. Throughout the Bible, God instructed people to tell their stories to their children.

As your kids get older, they are going to ask you straight, pointed questions. "Why should I believe what you believe? How do you know it's the Word of God? What makes you so sure?" The answer is not, "Because I said so" or even "Because the Bible says so." Don't get me wrong. The Bible is crucial to our belief system and is our guide, the inerrant Word of God. But your answer is in the stories, the experiences you've had that have proven Christ real in your life.

The same goes for the 20-something generation. They are a skeptical bunch. They aren't going to believe just because you tell them "it's the right thing." They will believe because they love and trust you, and they see it lived out in your life. They will believe because they've heard it in the stories you've told them of Christ's faithfulness in your life. They will believe because they continue to see Christ working in and through you before their eyes.

⚹ Free to be me! ⚹

Younger women will only see Christ if you let them get close enough to see who you really are. Why is this so hard? Because we have come to believe and accept things that are just not true. You've got to embrace the freedom

Christ has offered you...*to be you.* To embrace this freedom, you must quit believing the lies the enemy wants you to believe. I call these lies the "Myths of Mentoring," and we'll get into those right now!

Myths of Mentoring

What happens when you receive one of those e-mails that claim gloom and doom, the virus of all ages, or bad luck forever "if you don't pass this on"? Your first thought is, "Can this be true?" Then with a little research (*very* little), you realize that the fear, anxiety, or whatever emotion was produced by the unsolicited e-mail was completely unwarranted. The e-mail was a lie. A fake. False. Not true. An urban legend. A scare tactic.

The same principle stands for the myths that freak us out about mentoring. Once you dig down below the surface, you realize there's nothing to fear at all. Let's take a look at the common myths of mentoring and discover the truth about each one.

Myth: I must be smart.

Truth: You must be willing to share what you already know. God has taught you tons of stuff along your journey. That's what you must be willing to share with whomever God puts in your path. So what if you don't have an IQ of 180? To be honest, most of the world wouldn't be able to connect with you if you did!

God created *you* as *you* so you can use your story to touch the lives of those that God connects you with. You just have to be ready and willing to see and seize the opportunity.

✳ Myth: It's very time consuming. ✳

Truth: You must be willing to open up your life and allow someone to come along with you. You've got to start seeing your life and your daily schedule as an avenue to build relationships. I've learned that nobody has time to actually mentor. I'm sure that is an overstatement, but generally true. To think that I have to add one more meeting to my schedule is just too much to handle, so therefore I don't.

Here's the thing: You don't have to add anything to your schedule! The way to think about mentoring the next generation is to *show* them, not *tell* them. They want to *see* Jesus in your life. They want to see you walk the walk not just talk the talk. So take them along with you. Take them through life with you.

This does two things. You can get accomplished what needs to be done in your world, *and* it satisfies the curiosity of younger women to find out if your words match up to your life.

When I started doing this years ago, I didn't think I was making a difference in the lives of young women. I certainly didn't think I was mentoring! I just thought I was hanging out with them and enjoying their company. But what I realized was that I was *showing* them Christ in my life and in my everyday world. They would go to the grocery store with me, or to the mall. They would travel with me to the airport or to an event. I asked them to go with me to church events or to family gatherings. I had them in my home while I was cooking supper and then invited them to join us for dinner.

What did this show a young woman? It showed her *all* of me. The good, bad, and ugly! It showed her how I responded when the clerk in the grocery store gave me the wrong change. It showed her how I responded when the guy, who was in way too big a hurry, cut me off on the freeway. She was with me when a woman in the park approached me in tears, talked with me about some trials at home and we all prayed together on the spot. Other times she would simply help me cook dinner and laughed with us at the dinner table.

She also saw me when my response was *not* like Christ. She listened when I talked to her about my anger…and then I apologized to her because it wasn't the right way to respond. And then we talked about what the right response *should* have been.

> *My relationship with Loisa evolved all on its own. In the midst of the day to day is where we do life together. In the midst of dishes, laundry, and children, a friendship was formed that I will treasure for the rest of my life. I have never really thought of myself as a mentor to her, but I guess, in a way, I am. It's funny. Looking back over the course of our relationship, I have wondered many times if I have gained more from it than she has. By listening to her heart time and time again, I became the student of a generation I knew very little about and built a friendship with an amazing lady. I really did have something to offer, not by appearing to have it all together, but by opening my heart and my home, with all its imperfections and struggles.*
>
> *Mary Beth Adams*
> *Conroe, Texas*

Basically, we think this is just everyday life…and it is. But when we live it with intentionality, with someone else, we are mentoring. We just hate calling it that!

Myth: Younger girls don't want to hang out with me!

Truth: This is totally untrue! Because of the way this generation was raised and the pattern of the previous generation, there is a *longing* to have the influence of older women in their lives. There are so many young women who have little or no relationship with their moms. Or even if they have great relationships with their mothers, a lot of the time they aren't living in the same cities or even states where their moms live.

I didn't know when I met Mary Beth that the relationship we would come to have would affect me so deeply. There has never been a day that we decided she was my mentor. It was never an assignment or a responsibility. In other words, she was never required to like me. Instead, I've realized as we have gone through life together that she loves me.

I'm single and at that 20-something stage of life where it feels like the world expects me to have everything figured out. I expect it of myself, too. But she doesn't expect it of me. She doesn't have it all figured out either. Instead, as life happens, we take it on together. I never hesitate to call her when the world seems to fall apart. She never hesitates to assure me nothing has fallen apart; that it's just my perspective for the moment. I couldn't ask for more than that.

At 25, when life is so up in the air, nothing does more good in my heart than having her tell me I'm all right. I can't express it really…what it means to have someone smile when they see me, hold me when I weep, tell me not to take myself so seriously, look me in the eyes and tell me I'm OK when I don't feel OK. Mary Beth loves me when she doesn't have to. That kind of love changes a person. And I will never be the same.

Loisa Wright
Mission Viejo, California

I recently had this conversation with one of the girls I hang out with on a regular basis. She has an amazing Christian mom who loves and supports her completely. She lives in the same town as her mom and is very close to her. She made this enlightening comment to me, "I love my mom, and I have no doubt she loves me and has my best in mind. But she *has* to love me…she's my mom! You *choose* to love me. There's a difference."

Wow! Out of the mouths of babes! There *is* a difference when someone chooses to love you. There is nothing comparable to a mother's love, don't misunderstand me. But it's something special when someone who is older and wiser chooses to come alongside you, invest in you, and love you unconditionally.

⚹ Myth: I need to know the Bible better. ⚹

Truth: You need to be willing and ready to share what you already have learned. Yes, we all need to continue growing and learning. Absolutely. But to decide not to invest in the next generation because we aren't Billy Graham isn't really acceptable. Think about it: Do you know the Bible better now than you did last year? What about now compared to two years ago? Or five years ago? If you've attended one or two church services, the answer should be yes! Absolutely. So share what you know. God has taught you more than you think. We tend to focus on what we don't know more than what we *do* know.

A few years ago, we tried to talk my parents into buying a computer. They were in their 60s at the time. There was no way they were going to buy one. Computers were too complex, too complicated, too scary! But they finally succumbed to the ongoing pressure we were dealing out. Once they got one, they started playing around on it. They realized that they knew enough to get started. And once they started, my dad got so excited about the possibilities that he drove into Austin multiple times for advanced software lessons. The transformation in my parents from absolutely being opposed to owning a computer to not being able to function *without* one happened within a relatively short period of time. And it was awesome to watch!

Here's the point: *They knew enough to get started. They tried, the fear went away, and they continued to learn along the way.* They use their computer daily, and they'll never go back.

Bottom line: We don't need to know everything about the Bible before we start sharing it with someone else. I know that's an amazing concept! Deep, huh? But we all have these thoughts! We think we have to be smarter, wiser, deeper, *and* have all of the spiritual gifts and disciplines active and vibrant in our lives before we can start investing in someone else. *Wrong!* Start now! God wants to use you just where you are. He'll teach you along the way.

⚡ Myth: I don't have any curriculum. ⚡

Truth: Your *life* is your curriculum. Earlier I mentioned that God wants to use your experiences…your successes…your failures…your hurts…your life. We'll look at this more closely later in this guide, but let me assure you, you have plenty of material to use to impact the life of someone else.

⚡ Myth: I don't have anything to offer. ⚡

Truth: You have everything to offer. You have your time, your love, your laughter, your skills, your experience, your knowledge, your hugs, your tears…*you!*

Isn't it so typical what Satan puts in our head? *I'm not good enough. I don't have anything to offer. I'm not smart enough. As soon as I memorize 27 verses of Scripture and read the whole New Testament, fast for 40 days, and attend 18 Bible studies…then I'll start mentoring someone.*

No! All of those thoughts are just smokescreens to get you to put off what God wants you to be doing now, every day. The thought that we don't have anything to offer is purely from Satan himself. He doesn't necessarily want you to think you're worthless; he just wants to convince you to wait. Don't act now because of…whatever. It doesn't matter what…*just wait!*

⚹ The truth about mentoring is… ⚹

Mentoring is a *lifestyle*, not a program. It is basically taking the relationships God has put in your life, recognizing the God moments, and intentionally sharing what God has taught you in those moments and circumstances.

So don't believe the myths. God never asks more of us than we can give. He asks us to give what we have. Nothing more. Nothing less. We just have to be willing to act on the moments he puts in front of us. We must show what we know. And we must be ready and willing to share what he has done in our lives with whomever he puts in our lives.

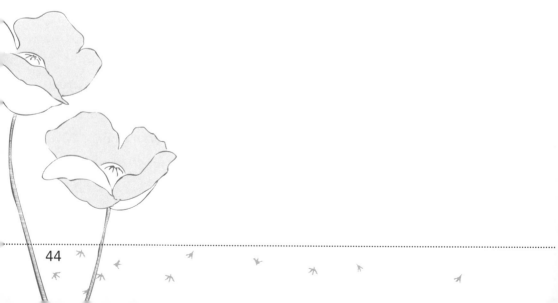

Change Your Lens!

A few years ago (I won't say how many) I turned 45. I found myself squinting at my computer and thought, "Oh my soul! I think I need some help here." So I went to the local drugstore and bought some reading glasses. About a week later, my husband and I were having a Bible study in our home, and when I opened my Bible I realized I couldn't even make out the words on the page. (Evidently the words must have shrunk.) I remembered the reading glasses. I put on the specs, looked at the page and, lo and behold, I could see! Hallelujah!

Here's the point:

The things that were right in front of me became clear when I was wearing the right lenses.

✶ ✶ ✶ ✶ ✶

In the same way that those glasses allowed me to see the words in my Bible and on my computer screen, changing your lens can help you to see the young women God has put, or is putting, in your path.

When I started seeing 20-somethings through a different lens, it was like becoming more aware of my surroundings. Kind of like when you buy a new car; suddenly you notice that model of car everywhere you go. Once I changed my lens, there were so many opportunities to become friends with and minister to these young women. The checkout girl at my supermarket, the girl at the coffee shop—the opportunity for ministry was all around me! It's been a true blessing in my life to have these relationships.

Kim Gore
Ladera Ranch, California

⚞ Where Are They? ⚟

So where can you find these next generation women? They're all around you! The babysitter, your best friend's daughter, the new college grad at work, a young mother who frequents the park where your kids play. Up to now, these young women have remained in your peripheral vision—noticed, appreciated, maybe even spoken to, but only as casual acquaintances. Change your lens. Could they benefit from a deeper relationship with you? Could you benefit from a deeper relationship with them? What steps can you take for the two of you to start building a more meaningful relationship? Here are a few ideas to get you started:

- Treat your babysitter to a special "thank you" lunch or coffee (in addition to her regular fee☺). Take some time to get to know her. Ask her what's going on in her life. Does she have another job? Is she in school?

- Does your friend's daughter seem to gravitate toward you? Have you had a significant conversation with her in the past? Go out to coffee.

Offer to help her decorate her apartment or house. Find out what she's interested in, and make a point to ask her about it; you could find you're interested too!

- Offer to help your newest colleague. Give her tips about the ins and outs of the office, and then invite her to lunch.

- Strike up a conversation with the woman at the park. Ask her about her kids and family. Set up a play date for your kids next week.

- Is there a young woman in your class at the gym that you always work out next to? Invite her for a smoothie after your workout.

- Do you know the name of the barista at your local coffee joint? Always be sure to ask how she is, and if she doesn't say "fine" or "good" take the time to follow up. (Don't forget to leave her a generous tip—she'll remember you!)

- You can also consider getting involved in a ministry at your church that naturally attracts 20-somethings. You can volunteer with MOPS, lead a small group for the college and career ministry, teach a Bible study for newlyweds with your spouse, or go on a mission trip, keeping your eye out for a young woman to connect with.

- Does the task seem too big to tackle alone? Get some friends to join in. Together you can plan events to invite 20-something women to attend (announce it in your church's bulletin or at the college ministry). Host a small cooking class at your home. You can all work together to make dinner and then sit down to a wonderful meal together.

- What kind of skill do you have that you could pass on to a group of young women? Maybe you're great at organization? Or perhaps you are the cooking queen. Do you like to walk dogs? Are you an athlete? Whatever it is, I'd be willing to bet that there is a younger woman who would love to learn from you.

✳ Pray! ✳

Above all else, the best tool at your disposal is prayer. Pray that God would open your eyes to the women walking in your path every day. And if there are no women in sight, pray and ask God to bring someone. He will be faithful to honor your request.

When I reflect on my life, I see that God has been putting young women and girls in my path all along. As my husband and I moved from church to church through Arkansas, Texas, New Mexico, and California, there were always young women that I hung out with. I never saw myself as their mentor but as their friend. I see now that through those friendships I was helping to disciple them. The stories I shared with them and the things they witnessed God doing in my life were helping them to grow in their own relationship with the Lord.

Looking back, I *wish* I had seen those moments through the lens of mentoring. I would have been more deliberate to share God moments. I would have been more intentional to point them to Scripture for answers. I would have been bolder when it came to stepping in at crucial times.

Remember, mentoring begins with friendship and is followed by spiritual investment. Like every good relationship, this one will take time to build trust. Stop looking for a ministry project and start looking for an honest, authentic relationship… one from which the two of you will learn and benefit.

Look around, take a risk, make the leap, and invite someone to walk with *you* today.

Women I might be mentoring…

Mentoring in Moments, Seasons, and for a Lifetime

I've learned that there are three different opportunities God gives us to mentor: in the moment, for a season, and for a lifetime. Every relationship begins with a moment, and for some, that's where it ends. But given some intentional time and energy that moment can blossom into a meaningful relationship. As you begin to change your lens, you'll start to see every interaction as an opportunity.

⊀ Mentoring in the Moments ⊀

True, today the greeting "How are you?" is more a courtesy than an inquiry into the state of someone's well-being, but that one question can open a lot of doors for mentoring moments. Again, it requires a change of lens to see that mentoring does not have to have a long-term commitment to have an impact. But you must be willing to take the extra few minutes to act on the opportunity God puts in front of you. So what does it look like to mentor in the moments?

A few months ago I was trying on some clothes in Target. As I entered the dressing room, I saw a young woman standing in front of the floor-length mirror in the hallway, turning from left to right, tilting her head, looking over her shoulder, attempting to view her outfit from every possible angle. I could see from the way she was analyzing her attire and practicing different looks in the mirror that this outfit was for something special.

"Those jeans look great on you," I said, in an aim to ease her anxiety just a bit.

"Really?" she questioned. "They're not too tight?"

From there I helped her explore some ensemble options from the clothes she'd brought in to try on. She told me about the young man she was going to see that night, how it was their first date, and she'd had a crush on him "like forever." She wanted to pick an outfit that was cute and flirty without being too suggestive. We found the perfect one! When she left she thanked me profusely for my help and seemed to be more excited than nervous.

Now I don't know this girl. I never even found out her name. I don't know if she's a Christian or if she goes to church. I'll probably never see her again, but in that moment I saw an opportunity to act in love, and I took advantage of it.

"So speak encouraging words to one another. Build up hope so you'll all be together in this, no one left out, no one left behind."
1 Thessalonians 5:11, The Message

It was just a moment, seemingly insignificant, but in that moment I was able to communicate Christ's love to a young girl. A girl who was in need of it. In need of encouragement, confidence, and a reminder of her beauty.

I saw that need and I attempted to meet it, scary as it was to put myself out there like that. Walking away that day, I realized that I left just as encouraged as she did.

Opportunities to communicate God's love and truth will be revealed to you if you ask him to open your eyes to them. Whether it's with a girl you see every day at the gym, a waitress at a restaurant you frequent, a checkout girl at the grocery store, someone who takes the same route on the bus or train during your morning commute, or even someone in the next dressing room. Don't waste a chance to connect with someone. You never know who may need just a little encouragement, and God can use *you* to make that happen!

⊁ Mentoring for a Season ⊀

Then there are times when God puts someone in your life for a little longer period of time…for a season. Maybe college is out, and a young girl starts working in your office for the summer; or maybe a newlywed joined your Bible study for the semester; or your kids are out of school, and you meet a young woman at the park whom you've never noticed before. These events may all have a limited timetable, but it also may be a time that God has purposefully put you in the position to be a young woman's friend.

Without recognizing that my new friend was 20-plus years younger than me, we started enjoying spending time together. It started as a casual acquaintance, but before I knew it, she was seeking me out. I realized God had planted her in my life and me in hers for a reason.

Mentor sounds like such a big-status name, but I guess that's what I am to her. I have walked where she hasn't yet walked. I have lived a life as a wife and mother that she hasn't yet lived.

Lindsey spends time with my family as if she is one of us. One of my favorite memories with Lindsey is having her over to my home and teaching her how to make coconut cream pies. We had so much fun!

She went to college, and I wasn't able to see her as much. But while she was there, we e-mailed and called to keep in touch. When she came home to visit, she always let me know she was in town so we could connect. She has actually moved back from college and will be attending school locally now, so I am looking forward to many days ahead of walking beside her as God leads both of us in life. Not only am I excited to see how God will work through me to help Lindsey, but I am also thrilled to see how God will work through Lindsey to speak to me. I pray our walk together will honor the Lord.

Sharla Ward
Amarillo, Texas

Sometimes we think that mentoring has to be this long, ongoing relationship, and sometimes it is. But sometimes, people enter our lives for short periods of time. Those short, seemingly insignificant connections could, very possibly, highly impact that young woman's life.

Once you've started seeing the people God puts in your path differently, you will see the opportunities he puts in front of you. We won't know the length of time we're supposed to be "something" to those people. We just need to be obedient and intentional in the moment, and let God do the rest!

When I think of mentoring in the seasons of my life, I think of two events that happened concurrently. It was our first pastorate in Danville, Arkansas, population 2,392. (Yes, that was the whole town.) So let me set the scene. Lance and I had been married five years and had just finished seminary at Criswell Seminary in Dallas. We moved from Dallas (big city), to Danville, Arkansas (total country), and lived on five acres of land behind the church. That five acres was surrounded by chicken farms.

Living on acreage versus living in a neighborhood is very different. Isolation is ever present. I didn't know a soul except the people at the church, and I didn't really know them…yet. My family lived 12 hours away in south Texas. Our church ran about 50 people. I was pregnant with Jonathan, my firstborn. And basically I was totally clueless about everything from being a pastor's wife and a mother, to living in the country, and dealing with isolation. It was quite a challenge, to say the least.

During those six years, two women took me under their wing, Sandra Moudy and Doris Majors. Sandra had kids that ranged in age from 4 to 8 years old. She immediately befriended me. We hung out at her house all of the time, and she helped me through the "baby" times. She showed me where shopping centers were and where to find the best deals on baby clothes. She helped me with discipline issues. I watched her with her kids. She loved them desperately but was firm and consistent with them. She loved her husband and he loved her. She let me see the times when she was frustrated with him. She let me know how they resolved their conflicts. It was an amazing and needed time of learning for me as a new mom and young wife.

Then there was Doris. She was a little further down the path than Sandy. She was more of a grandma to my son, Jonathan. But what I remember about our relationship is that she was always teaching me something. She taught me how to can pickles and to bake bread. She was always "putting up" something, which I figured out meant canning. She was a true Proverbs 31 woman. She was always busy. She was working with her husband in their business, working in her garden, or working in her kitchen. She always had time for me when I would call her up with a canning question. Sometimes she'd say, "Why don't you just come over and I'll show you." Wow! I loved that!

But what both of these women probably don't realize is the spiritual influence they had on me. They both truly lived out their faith daily. Both Sandy and Doris loved the Lord, and it showed up in the everyday things they did. And as I walked with them through everyday life, I saw Jesus in their lives. They shared stories of what Christ had done in their lives. I watched them as they'd look up the Scripture that had touched them that day and read it to me. They were Jesus with skin on for a season of time, a crucial season of life for me!

At the same time Sandy and Doris were mentoring me, God put Debbie in my life. I was only 25 at the time and she was in high school. She started going to our church, and we struck up a friendship. She would drop by the house and help me with newborn Jonathan. She helped me fold clothes and cook supper. But during the years we were in Arkansas, Debbie had some tragic things happen in her life, and she turned to us for answers. The answers she wanted, we couldn't give her. We didn't give her the cliché answers that come so easily: "Everything happens for the good"; "God's timing is perfect"; "We don't see what he sees"; "They're in a better place." No! We loved and supported her through these times. We cried with her and held her when she needed someone. We tried to help her family when they were hurting. Our words were basically meaningless during those times, but our actions were priceless.

I haven't talked to or seen any of these women for years, but they were all instrumental early on in my life. I don't think any of us would have thought that what we were doing was mentoring. But I can say, without a doubt, it was! They all helped me see how mentoring at the most elementary level can be so deeply effective.

We don't know how long seasons of mentoring will be. The point is to be obedient. Be whom God wants you to be for however long he wants you to be. The young woman you see may only be in your life for a few weeks, months, or maybe a year, but what rubs off on her in that time period may be life changing. You may be the first authentic Christian she's ever met. You may be the first person who's had a meaningful conversation with her since she's moved there. Or maybe she's just having a tough time in general and has no one to process with. When you make yourself available to listen, hear, and give personal, God-honoring advice, you are being Jesus with skin on.

"He comes alongside us when we go through hard times, and before you know it, he brings us alongside someone else who is going through hard times so that we can be there for that person just as God was there for us. We have plenty of hard times that come from following the Messiah, but no more so than the good times of his healing comfort—we get a full measure of that, too."

2 Corinthians 1:4-5, The Message

⚹ Mentoring for a Lifetime ⚹

Let me start by saying that lifetime mentoring relationships are few and far between, even rare. But when you take the time to recognize and cultivate them, they are invaluable for her *and* you!

Cathi is one of these relationships in my life. We don't meet every week or go through studies together. But we have a long-term relationship that is ongoing.

In the many years I've known Cathi, she has watched me go through all sorts of seasons and events—a lifetime's worth, in fact. She's been alongside me through some of life's most pivotal moments. She was there when my daughter graduated from high school, when my son moved out, and for both of their weddings. She watched and prayed with my husband and me as we made life-changing decisions regarding work and ministry. She's seen the whole gamut of my emotions; from the depths of depression to the heights of elation. She's seen me make choices in the flesh and when I've set myself in the center of God's will. Together we've belly laughed and had difficult discussions, some resulting in tears.

Just like any relationship, ours has changed and evolved over time. She's grown in her confidence and ability to make wise choices on her own. While she doesn't run everything by me, I know that our relationship is helping her to make these decisions. When I listen to Cathi talk, there are phrases she uses and things she says that I know she has picked up from listening to and walking with me. I know she sees marriage and family differently because she has watched my marriage and my family. I know she sees ministry differently because of what she's seen in our lives. I've seen God work in her life as she's seen him work in my life. But she never would have seen him in my life if I hadn't let her into my life. As we've walked together, she's seen that my relationship with Christ is real, not just words or a Sunday-morning outing.

Mentoring for a lifetime means simply making your life available.

It means intentionally investing enough time in and with someone that it shapes her for a lifetime. Allowing someone to observe and even participate in the ins and outs of marriage, parenting, and career, and coupling that with a knowledge of God to ensure that she has the wisdom and experience to make wise choices in her own life, *whether you're with her or not.* I believe that Cathi and I will be in each other's lives for the long haul, but if that were to change, I'm confident that she's seen enough of my life to carry her through whatever comes her way.

Mentoring is not a commitment to a length of time; it's a commitment to a way of life.

I don't think anybody ever told me I was going to be Ryanne's mentor. There was no official start to our relationship. It started off and continues to be very casual. She was a student in our youth ministry, and I was an adult leader. Truth is I liked her and wanted to spend more time with her. She was fun, energetic, and well...a freshman in high school. She and her friends reminded me of what I was like in high school.

As time passed our relationship grew, and we began to invite each other into the events of our personal lives. Some were very exciting like her senior prom; others were just everyday life, like shopping at Target for home decorations for my new house. We just began to "do life" with one another. I told her about what was happening in my life and would ask her what was happening in her life. I made an effort to celebrate the moments in her life that I remembered marked who I was and had become. Things like getting her driver's license, going away to college, birthdays, boyfriends—all the things that life revolves around when you are young. In the midst of these moments, I would look for ways and find opportunities to encourage and challenge her faith.

As the years passed my life was changing. I was getting married, having babies, and God was at work in my life in big and little ways. Through it all, I would share with Ryanne what I was learning. I would share what was hard (maybe because of mistakes from my past) and what was rewarding because of some good habits and boundaries I had put in place. All of this was modeling my faith and spiritual journey to Ryanne, and little did I know, it was shaping her as well.

Last year Ryanne got married and I had the privilege of being her matron of honor. As I was thinking about the significant role she was allowing me to play in her wedding, I couldn't help but think of the significant role she had been playing in my life. She had become like a little sister to me—someone whom I loved very much, someone whom I wanted to protect, someone whom I wanted to encourage, spend time with, journey with, and experience life and faith with. Ryanne and I have become more than friends. She is part of my family and hopefully will be part of my life forever.

Jana Sarti
Foothill Ranch, California

The young woman Jana was investing in is now my daughter-in-law. Was Jana's investment valuable? I would say, *absolutely!*

I wasn't looking for someone to pour into my life. It just happened. Jana was someone I had crossed paths with that was a little bit older and showed interest in my life and decisions. She never told me how to make a decision, but she always shared with me what life lessons she had learned. The most important thing was that she chose to "do life" with me. She chose to let me in the ins and outs of her everyday life. It started with us going out to lunch, and soon we were spending all kinds of time together. Usually whatever we were doing wasn't super exciting—walking down the aisles at the grocery store, driving to the airport to pick up a friend of hers—but it was always filled with great conversations and lots of laughter. Soon it seemed like we made memories no matter what we were doing. We could be sitting on the couch watching TV or going on a road trip, but either way we were together!

Sometimes Jana had to speak truth into my life that I didn't want to hear or that hurt my feelings, but it always came down to her having a similar experience and wanting to save me from making any unnecessary mistakes. Even though it may not have happened in that exact moment, there was always forgiveness and explanation—and our bond became stronger!

Then out of the blue, I had an "aha" moment in which I realized after many years of friendship and mentorship, Jana had become my family. The funny thing is it had seemed like it was always that way, and I wasn't sure if it had ever been any different. Nowadays we are on much more of a friend level, but Jana has played many roles in my life: mentor, big sister, boss, and landlord! I am still learning from Jana every day. She is still allowing me to peer into her life as she is a wife, a mom, a daughter, an aunt, and a strong Christian woman! And last year, just as I had taken a part in her wedding, I made sure the day that I said "I do," she was standing right next to me as my matron of honor (even if she was nine-months pregnant!). It is so exciting to be able to be in a new chapter of my life knowing that Jana is looking out for me, praying for me, and loving on me and my husband whenever she can. I can't imagine "doing life" without her!

Ryanne Witt
Rancho Santa Margarita, California

The bottom line is this: Be aware of those God puts in your life. He has or *will* send someone into your life. If it's just for a moment, seize that moment. If it's for a season, recognize the opportunity and relish that time. And if God blesses you with a lifelong friend and companion, dive in and open your life to her. You won't be sorry you did!

Why?
The Bible Tells Me So!

So why is *lifestyle mentoring* the mentoring model for the next generation? First, it's the model that the next generation will respond to: relationship versus program. Second, and more important, because throughout all of Scripture this model is exhibited. From Moses to Joshua, Paul to Timothy, and most important from Jesus to his followers; the older generations pass along the stories of God's love, his Word, and his faithfulness to the younger generations. It is not only modeled, but commanded.

"Attention, Israel! God, our God! God the one and only! Love God, your God, with your whole heart: love him with all that's in you, love him with all you've got! Write these commandments that I've given you today on your hearts. Get them inside of you and then get them inside your children. Talk about them wherever you are, sitting at home or walking in the street; talk about them from the time you get up in the morning to when you fall into bed at night. Tie them on your hands and foreheads as a reminder; inscribe them on the doorposts of your homes and on your city gates...

"The next time your child asks you, 'What do these requirements and regulations and rules that God, our God, has commanded mean?' tell your child, 'We were slaves to Pharaoh in Egypt and God powerfully intervened and got us out of that country. We stood there and watched as God delivered miracle-signs, great wonders, and evil-visitations on Egypt, on Pharaoh and his household. He pulled us out of there so he could bring us here and give us the land he so solemnly promised to our ancestors. That's why God commanded us to follow all these rules, so that we would live reverently before God, our God, as he gives us this good life, keeping us alive for a long time to come.'"

Deuteronomy 6:4-9, 20-24, The Message

⊁ You have a story to share ⊀

"Attention, Israel! God, our God! God the one and only! Love God, your God, with your whole heart: love him with all that's in you, love him with all you've got! Write these commandments that I've given you today on your hearts. Get them inside of you and then get them inside your children."

As Israel is being established as a nation (a pivotal point in God's story), God gives his people this command. He does not reserve it for Moses on top of Mount Sinai or for Aaron and those in the priesthood (the pastors and leaders of the church so to speak). No! God addresses the nation of Israel, *all* who had seen his mighty works in freeing them from Egypt. The tent makers, the mothers, the carpenters, the shepherds—*all* who had partaken in his goodness in the desert. They all had a story to tell, just as you have a story to tell of God's goodness in your life.

⚹ Wherever you are ⚹

"Talk about them *wherever you are, sitting at home or walking in the street; talk about them from the time you get up in the morning to when you fall into bed at night.* Tie them on your hands and foreheads as a reminder; inscribe them on the doorposts of your homes and on your city gates" (italics added).

From the time you wake until you fall asleep at night your life is a testimony to Christ's work. Driving to the grocery store, playing with your kids, eating dinner with your family are all opportunities to pass along your faith experience to someone. Perhaps that someone wasn't blessed to grow up in a Christian home, or maybe they just need a new perspective on God and the Christian life. *Wherever you are,* whatever you are doing, the opportunity is there for God moments to happen. You just have to recognize them and be ready to respond in those moments.

⚹ Passing it on ⚹

"*…tell your child,* `We were slaves to Pharaoh in Egypt and God powerfully intervened and got us out of that country. We stood there and watched as God delivered miracle-signs, great wonders, and evil-visitations on Egypt, on Pharaoh and his household. He pulled us out of there so he could bring us here and give us the land he so solemnly promised to our ancestors. That's why God commanded us to follow all these rules, so that we would live reverently before God, our God, as he gives us this good life, keeping us alive for a long time to come'" (italics added).

Don't wait for Sunday morning, don't rely on a Bible study, no need to wait for the DVD curriculum, or enroll in seminary. Your greatest teaching tool is your life, your story of God's salvation. What better evidence do we have? What stronger testimony to his commandments than when we are obedient and we experience his goodness? Or when we are disobedient and we experience his grace and forgiveness? Don't underestimate the work that God has done in your life or the power of your story.

The women you mentor will feel closer to you and closer to the Lord as a result of you passing it on. They will believe because they've seen Christ in you. They will believe because they've heard the stories you've told them of Christ's faithfulness in your life. They will believe because they continue to see Christ working in and through you as they walk with you through life.

✳ Jesus Mentored in the Moments ✳

Now consider the ministry of Jesus. He took the time to mentor in the moments, the seasons, and for his lifetime. He never seemed to be too busy to notice a person or the need of a person.

He seized the opportunity to speak to the woman at the well. John 4 recounts the story of Jesus taking a detour through Samaria and talking to a woman there. This woman was a known adulteress. Jesus was tired and thirsty. But he didn't let these things get in the way of passing along his knowledge of God's love and the life he had available to this hurting woman.

What about the time Jesus was teaching and the paralytic was lowered through the roof and Jesus healed him? What about Zacchaeus and Nicodemus? What about the woman who touched his robe? With all of these people, Jesus stopped and noticed...in the moment!

✳ Jesus Mentored in the Seasons ✳

Jesus' ministry as a whole was basically a season. It was only three years. But during those three years, he spent time with people, both momentarily and extensively. His entire life was punctuated with stories. He took the time to talk with people. He listened and cared. He used parables to get a point across. He told stories to masses and individuals. And when people heard him speak, they were so moved, they told others of what they had heard and learned, and they were changed forever.

The disciples were so convinced of his deity that they spent the rest of their lives speaking of him, living for him, and ultimately dying for him.

✳ Jesus Mentored for a Lifetime ✳

Jesus relished the time he spent with his disciples. They ate together, traveled together, prayed together, and wept together. Throughout the three years of Jesus' ministry, he lived with these younger men, passing along his knowledge of the Kingdom, teaching them the ways of his Father, and empowering them to do ministry in the community. The disciples watched Jesus' ministry so closely that they were able to continue the work that he started after his death and resurrection, proclaiming the coming of the Kingdom and salvation for all those who called on his name. How did they know how to heal the sick? To cast out demons? By watching and learning from their teacher, Jesus.

"Then he appointed twelve of them and called them his apostles. They were to accompany him, and he would send them out to preach."
Mark 3:14

He spent enough time with his disciples that they saw the authenticity in his life and his passion for his Father. They saw him laugh and cry, heal the sick, care for the hurting, laugh with friends, and cry in anguish in the Garden of Gethsemane. They saw him play with the children and eat dinner with a tax collector! They saw him minister to a prostitute and hang out with fishermen. They watched him live out the things he was trying to teach them. And because of his love for his Father and the "realness" in which he loved each of them, they took on his characteristics and his mission. They saw his deity up close and personal.

⚹ This is bigger than you! ⚸

Which leads me to this thought: *This is bigger than you.* Mentoring is more than cooking lessons, child-rearing tips, and a shopping buddy, though all of those things are truly important. Mentoring is about passing on the story of your life, with God as the central character. True, there will be times when he doesn't feel central. He may feel distant and at times nonexistent. It may seem that you, your problems, or your fears have taken center stage. But no matter what your "feeling" about him is in the moment, you must realize that communicating an ever-increasing desire to draw close to him, depend on him, and trust him *regardless* of our feelings is a message the next generation desperately needs to hear.

"You have heard me teach things that have been confirmed by many reliable witnesses. Now teach these truths to other trustworthy people who will be able to pass them on to others."
2 Timothy 2:2

The values, history, and stories of God were passed on life to life. They were passed on as people walked down the road with their kids. They were passed on as they were sitting around the fire at night, drinking coffee (or whatever they drank!). Stories of God's miracles; stories of Abraham, Isaac, and Jacob; stories of captivity, deliverance, famine, and feast; all were passed on from families to tribes to the nation of Israel until the time of Jesus. And after the resurrection, stories of Christ's healing and miracles, his grace, and the forgiveness available through him were passed on by the disciples, shaping the Christian world with their eyewitness accounts of the long-awaited Messiah, passed from generation to generation until the story reached your ears.

The story is not over. Each of us has a chapter to contribute, and most important, to pass on. These stories will touch the lives and hearts of future generations, if only we'd be willing to share what God has done in us. *That* is what mentoring is today—sharing the story of God and how he's worked in our life with those he puts in our path.

> *I met Erin at a gathering in my home when she was 19 years old. She wanted to be in a small group with some older, wiser women and was ultimately looking for a mentor. Little did I know that within the next year, I would become that mentor.*
>
> *We both agreed that we did not need to do another study. So we decided to get together, talk about life, and take it from there. And that's what we did. I realized that while we were running errands, she observed how I handled money and how I made everyday decisions and choices. We talked about relationships and handling conflict. We talked about having faith in all situations whether big or small. It was amazing how God would bring to mind something he had taught me, sometimes long ago, to share with her. He always gave me just the right words at the right moment.*
>
> *Today Erin is 25. I had the privilege of being her matron of honor when she was married last month. To stand by her side as she took this big step is a highlight of my life.*

Now I'm a "grand mentor." Erin is investing in a 14-year young lady named Margaret. It's exciting to see how God is using some of the things I've passed on to Erin to influence Margaret. How humbling! I don't have biological children, but I can say without a doubt that I have a spiritual daughter. I am grateful for the legacy that I'll leave through her and count it a privilege to call her friend.

Deanne Brewer
San Diego, California

OK...but How?

What Do I Have to Offer?

What a loaded question! You have so much to offer, and if you're like me, you don't even realize it. Let's look at what you've got to offer!

✳ Your Experiences ✳

Sharing your experiences, your story, with younger women is the key to relationship. Throughout the Bible, God instructed people to tell their children stories. Jesus continuously talked to and communicated with people through stories. He taught his disciples as they walked down the road.

Remember—

You impress from a distance, but you impact up close and personal.

Think of all the experiences you've had in your life: the good and the bad that younger women could learn from. Did you go to college, get married, have children, move to a new town, or begin a new job? Did you battle depression; battle an illness; get into debt; lose a parent, a friend, or a child; lose a job; struggle with infertility; go through a breakup or get divorced? Younger women are facing similar things, and hearing your story, how you got through it, hearing what God taught you through it and continues to teach you, can help them. Just having your support can be a tremendous help to them. Whether you handled these seasons with grace or made some royal mistakes, you have something of value to share with the next generation.

God can speak to others through the experiences, the successes, the failures, the loves and hurts you've gone through in your life. Through your spiritual journey!

⚹ Your Successes ⚹

Certainly you do some things better than anyone else! We all have areas of strength and success. Sharing the successes in your life gives hope to the next generation. Even if the path to the success was hard and filled with potholes, that story in itself holds encouragement to the next generation.

⚹ Your Failures ⚹

Sharing failures with the next generation helps make us real. It helps them see that your life, which might appear relatively great or successful, has had ups and downs. Hearing your story, all of it, good *and* bad, helps them to realize that it's not the end of the world when *they* fail. It's part of the journey. And it makes us who we are. It is what God uses to shape us into who he wants us to be.

⚹ Your Hurts ⚹

Life doesn't always turn out the way we think. Things happen…some joyous, some difficult, some seemingly unbearable. But the fact remains that God is faithful to bring us through even the most trying of times, and he does so, so that we might pass on news of his faithfulness to others.

"He comes alongside us when we go through hard times, and before you know it, he brings us alongside someone else who is going through hard times so that we can be there for that person just as God is there for us. We have plenty of hard times that come from following the Messiah, but no more so than the good times of his healing comfort—we get a full measure of that, too."

2 Corinthians 1:4-5, The Message

God can use your hurts to show others your vulnerability. Being vulnerable with someone is the quickest way for her to become vulnerable with you. The more you give emotionally, the more you get in return. The more you share, the more people will open up to you. To help younger women, you must be willing to come clean and show that you have been on the hurting end of things. You can't keep the "everything is fabulous" face on all of the time…nor should you!

⚹ Your Spiritual Journey ⚹

So how will they see Christ in your life? By sharing with them the journey that God has brought you on, the story he's telling through your life. This is where the rubber meets the road. Consider how God has worked in your life over the years, the lessons you've learned, the ways you've grown, the times you've taken two steps back. What are verses that have carried you through? Who are people that have prayed for you and supported you? What messages did God give others to speak into your life? These are all a part of your spiritual journey, and they are there for you to share with a younger woman.

These are the things you share with those God puts in your path. See? You definitely have much more to share with others than you think! God has taught you tons of things! He's given you lots of opportunities to learn. You just need to recognize when God gives you the opportunity to share those moments with others and act on it.

So this is your curriculum: your experiences, successes, failures, hurts, and your spiritual journey. These are the things that impact other people. These are the things that will impact the next generation. Your life touching other lives!

So let's get specific.

Think about it...

Sometimes it's hard to think of things that God can use in your life. Use these questions and "nudges" to think through your journey and see how God has used what you've gone through to make you who you are today. Then take those experiences and pass them on. We encourage you to write down your findings. You will be encouraged and blessed when you look back over your notes and see how God has worked in your life. So get out a pen, and let's begin!

Experiences

• What have been the major milestones in your life so far?

....

....

....

....

• What are some of the biggest adventures you've had, and what did you learn through them?

....

....

....

• List some positive experiences in your life.

....

....

....

• List a few negative experiences.

....

....

....

• Who were the people that were most influential in your life? Were they influential for a moment, a season, or a lifetime?

....

....

....

• What were the big, major events or decisions that changed the direction your life was going in? Did your life change for better or for worse?

....

....

....

....

Successes

• What are you passionate about?

....

....

....

....

• What things do you simply *love* to do?

....

....

....

....

• In what areas of your life have you excelled? (Don't be shy. This is the time to brag!)

  • Job/Career

  • Arts/Creativity

  • Listening

- Encouraging

- Painting

- Setting a budget

- Cleaning

- ....

- ....

- ....

- ....

- What about other achievements? Sports? Awards? Trophies? Academics?

....

....

....

....

- What have you physically done that you consider an accomplishment? Run a marathon? Flipped a house? Organized your closet?

....

....

....

....

- What everyday skills can you pass on? Can you fold laundry well? (You'd be surprised how many 20-somethings can't fold laundry!) Do you make the world's best pie crust? Balance a checkbook in five minutes flat? What other hidden talents do you have?

....

....

....

....

• How have you handled success?

....

....

....

....

• What has God taught you through your successes?

....

....

....

....

Failures

Are there things in your life that have shaped you because of failure in those areas? Have you had failures in one or more of the following areas? If so, how have these failures shaped you? What else could you add to this list?

• Friendships

• Marriage/Relationships with men

• Parenting

• School

• Job

• Ministry

• Finances

• ....

• ....

• ....

• What are some choices you've made in the past that you'd like a "do-over" on?

....
....
....
....

• What have you learned through these failures?

....
....
....
....

• How have you dealt with your failures?

....
....
....
....

• What has God taught you through these experiences?

....
....
....
....

• How have you experienced God's grace?

....
....
....
....
....

Hurts

- How have you been hurt in the past?

....
....
....
....
....

- What are some painful experiences that have shaped your life? Illness? Loss of a child, a spouse, or a parent?

....
....
....
....
....

- Who has hurt you?

  - Employers

  - Friends

  - Family

  - ....

  - ....

- How do those hurts affect your "trust-o-meter"?

....
....
....
....
....

• How do those hurts affect your faith?

....
....
....
....

• Have you gotten over and through those hurts, or are you still dealing with them?

....
....
....
....

• What have you learned from your hurtful experiences?

....
....
....
....

• How have your hurts changed your relationships?

....
....
....
....

• How have you grown through hurtful experiences?

....
....
....
....

• What have you learned about dealing with people who have hurt you?

....

....

....

....

....

Spiritual Journey

Looking back over the topics that we've covered, where do you see God's hand? Ask yourself these questions:

• How did you come to have a relationship with Jesus?

....

....

....

....

....

• How do you connect with God regularly?

....

....

....

....

....

• How do you learn spiritual lessons—through people, Scripture, a song, a sermon, prayer? All of the above?

....

....

....

....

- What experiences made you turn to God or draw closer to him?

....

....

....

....

- When have you felt distant from God?

....

....

....

....

- What is your relationship with God right now, honestly?

....

....

....

....

- When have you gone through a spiritually dry patch, and how did that feel? How did you get through that time?

....

....

....

....

- What is God teaching you right now?

....

....

....

....

• What softens your heart toward him—people, music, nature, solitude?

....
....
....
....

• What Bible verses are most meaningful to you? Why?

....
....
....
....

Along with what God has taught you through the experiences in your life, think about this…

• How many sermons have you heard, and how many Bible studies have you listened to? (Not that the actual number matters, but you've certainly picked up a few things from all those sermons and studies!)

• How many retreats have you gone to?

• How many times have you had a quiet time?

• What has God taught you in your quiet times?

• How did he speak to you?

• What verses have been meaningful to you?

• How has God answered your prayers?

• What is a specific prayer that you know God answered?

God used all of these things to shape you into who you are today. And he will continue to shape you. So take a chance! Share what he's taught you to impact someone he has put in your path. Your journey is full of lessons she needs to learn, too!

Your Calendar

Most mentoring programs have you set a specific day and time to meet every week. Although this may have worked for some in the past, young women today are wired very differently. They have short attention spans and are more apt to do something on the fly than on a planned schedule.

The answer is mentoring "as you go." When God puts a young woman in your life, instead of meeting her every week at the coffee bar, take her along with you. When you start thinking in these terms, everything is a ministry moment. These are the times when she watches you. When your 2-year-old throws a conniption fit in the middle of Target, how do you respond? When you get the phone call that you need an appointment with a teacher, this young woman is listening. She watches you when your husband calls and asks you to do him "a favor," which takes an hour and a half out of your day and puts you that much further behind. These are the "life moments" where she watches how you live out your Christian walk.

These are also the times when the conversations come up about struggles she's having. How does she deal with her temptation? What should she do about a relationship? How should she go about addressing an issue? These conversations don't happen at church. They happen as relationships go deeper and trust is built. As you let her in, she will let you in.

This is an awesome concept when you think about it! You don't have to add another thing to your schedule, you can get your to-do list done, *and* you can mentor in the process. It's the way Christ did it! He was never too busy to speak to someone in need.

So we've included a couple of mock schedules. Look at each calendar with the question, "Could I take someone with me to do this?" Use this calendar as an example to start thinking of ways you can have someone come alongside you and watch you "as you go."

Calendar of a 9-to-5 Career Gal

Monday	Tuesday	Wednesday	Thursday	Friday	Saturday	Sunday
7-8 Gym	7-8 Gym	7-8 Gym	7-8 Gym	7-8 Gym	9 Walk the lake	8:30-12 Church
9-5 Office	9-5 Office	9-5 Office	9-5 Office	9-5 Office	10-1 Errands & lunch	2-5 Barbecue with friends
6-7:30 Dinner	6-9 Dinner & movie	12-1 Meet friend for lunch	6-7 Dinner	7-9 Theater	5:30-7 Cook my favorite dinner	
		6-7 Dinner	8-10 TV favorites night			

Calendar of a Stay-at-Home Gal

Monday	Tuesday	Wednesday	Thursday	Friday	Saturday	Sunday
9-10 Gym	8 Drop kids at school	7:30 Gym	9 Shopping & lunch	7:30 Gym	10 Yardwork	9:30-1 Church & lunch
10-11:30 Laundry/ housework	1:30 Pedicure	12 Lunch	3:30 Pick up kids	9 Laundry/ housework	12 Lunch	1 Walk
12-1 Lunch	2:30 Grocery shopping	1:00 Haircut	7:30 Kids: homework & bed	12 Lunch	1:30 Soccer game	2:30 Movie during sports
3:30-4 Pick up kids	3:30-4 Pick up kids	3:30-4 Pick up kids		3:30-4 Pick up kids	5 Family birthday party	6 Dinner with family
6-7 Dinner with family	4:30 Soccer practice	7:30-8:30 Kids: homework & bed		4 Kids: ice cream & park		
7:30-8:30 Kids: homework & bed				6 Dinner & movie		

Now review your own schedule. Here's a blank calendar to help you get started. Fill in your standing commitments, and look for opportunities to have someone come alongside you and live life with you "as you go"!

Monday	Tuesday	Wednesday	Thursday	Friday	Saturday	Sunday

Things to Do...Together

You might be thinking, "OK, I've found a young woman I'd like to share my life with...but now what do we do?"

Here are a few ideas to get you started. Put a check mark by the ones you could put into action in your own life.

1. Take a walk.

2. Go to the gym.

3. Have her join you when you pick up your kids from school.

4. Go to the park with your kids.

5. Grab a cup of coffee or an ice-cream cone.

6. Go to lunch.

7. Do you need to bake cupcakes for your kid's class? Do it together!

8. Go shopping.

9. Help her decorate her apartment.

10. Teach her to cook your dinner specialty.

11. Have an at-home movie night.

12. Go to the movies.

13. Join a Bible study together.

14. Go to church together.

15. Meet her on her lunch break.

16. Watch your and/or her favorite show.

17. Go to a bookstore.

18. Help her plan a special night for the special someone in her life.

19. Go to the pet store. (Who doesn't love puppies?)

20. Celebrate holidays.

21. Go to the grocery store.

22. Do you need a housesitter? Why not ask her?

23. Show up for her special events.

24. Try out a new restaurant together.

25. Join a ministry together.

26. Get a pedicure.

27. Go to a sporting event.

28. Take her to the airport. Or have her take you.

29. Family days…take her along!

30. Have her over in the evenings, and let her watch what reality is!

31. Have her over if she has an afternoon off.

32. Take her magazines and chicken soup when she's sick.

33. If she needs to meet with her friends and they can't find a place, offer your home.

34. Help her clean her apartment.

35. Surprise her with little gifts you know she loves (even if they're out of your comfort zone).

36. Ask her to teach you to do something she does well—you might learn a new skill!

⚹ Are you technologically challenged? ⚹

1. Have her teach you how to text message.

2. Do you have an iPod? Get one! They're awesome! Then have her teach you how to use it.

3. Download music that she likes, and talk about the genre.

4. Ask her what a genre is! ☺

5. Ask her about starting a blog for your family.

6. Do you need some help with your computer? Ask her!

7. Talk to her about the perks and dangers of MySpace or Facebook. Then have her teach you to set up your own page on one of these!

Can you think of other things that you could do together? Write them down here:

....

....

....

....

....

....

....

....

....

....

Marks of Mentoring

Now, you've found a younger woman, you're spending time together, and sharing your life. What else? Here are my ten commandments (so to speak) of mentoring. These are foundational elements and powerful tools for you to remember and use. They aren't hard or time consuming, but without them, you will be ineffective.

☀ 1. You must be authentic. ☀

Be *real*! Earlier, I talked about what type of people we all are more comfortable being around…those with flaws or those that have everything totally together. Whichever category you are in, the flawed or unflawed, the main thing you have to be is *real*. You must be who you are. The lovely *and* the unlovely. The happy or sad, contemplative, or mad…whatever. Be what and who you are.

Now you may need to go back and fess up to not acting Christ-like in some moments. But those are great teaching times on tons of levels. A younger woman may have never seen someone your age apologizing to someone her age. She may have never seen anyone apologize, period! It gives you the opportunity to have a great conversation about what you should have done, how Jesus would have reacted. It will show her you can still be a Christian, love the Lord, and mess up!

2. Listen and learn.

We don't have to have all the answers. In fact, we don't have to have hardly any of the answers. But we must learn to listen. Listen and hear what these younger women are saying.

Listening and hearing are not the same. There may be an underlying guilt or anger issue with the girl in your life. There might be underlying family issues or sexual issues. She needs someone to talk to. Some girls have no one to talk with except people their own age. While that is helpful, it isn't always the best advice. And there are definitely some things girls don't want to talk about with their parents.

Be sensitive to know when you need to seek help. Don't get in over your head. If there are issues that are beyond your scope of advice, volunteer to go with her to meet with a counselor. In fact, this book includes a list of things that are helpful to know about the girls you invest in. This list will help you know a young woman's background better so you will be able to understand where she's coming from and pray for her in a clearer, more specific way.

3. Maintain confidentiality.

This is a non-negotiable. This generation is adult-wary anyway. They definitely do not need to confide in an adult only to have that person turn around and tell someone else. If you feel there is an issue that you need someone else's input on, ask her if it would be OK for you to get some advice from a couple of other people. She will be so grateful that you asked for her permission. And as an extra bonus, her respect for you will go up considerably.

4. Ask the right questions.

Asking questions is the quickest way to get to know someone. People love to talk about themselves. But remember, 20-somethings are already a little skittish when it comes to their "elders." But having someone a generation or two older than them be genuinely interested in them is inviting. The key word here is *genuinely*. So when cultivating a relationship with the next generation, the gift of listening is invaluable.

Ask questions that dig deeper. Choose questions that will help her see what's really going on and also see different ways to figure out what the right response to an issue is. What are the underlying issues? What is driving some of her opinions, attitudes, actions? You don't have to make her feel like you're grilling her, but ask questions that matter.

5. Follow up and follow through.

Let's do lunch!

I'd love to get together!

I'll be praying for you!

These are statements we use on a regular basis. Unfortunately, these phrases often are flippant comments rather than genuine commitments. Even with good intentions, the principle of "out of sight, out of mind" prevails. We walk away from these conversations and don't think about them again.

In lifestyle mentoring, following up and following through are key. Let me illustrate. Let's say God has put a young woman in your life. You start to make intentional efforts to connect with her. She talks with you on a Sunday morning about a job interview she's going to have that week. You tell her you'll be praying for her about the interview and the direction she should take concerning this job.

Follow through. Do whatever it takes to remind yourself to pray for her! Write it on a sticky note. Mark it on your calendar. Send yourself an e-mail. No matter what it takes, pray for her! Pray for God's wisdom, for calmness, and for confidence. Then send her an e-mail or text message the night or morning before her interview to let her know you're thinking about her and praying for her.

Follow up. After the interview, send her a note or call her to ask how it went. Give her space and time to respond, but let her know she's on your heart and that you care about what God's doing in her life.

These things seem so simple. They don't take a lot of time and effort, but they go a long way toward building and strengthening a relationship. Keep in touch and keep your word. Both are critical to building relationships in general, and with this generation, even more so!

⚹ 6. Encouragement is key. ⚹

Always, always encourage. If you think the decision she is planning on making is not the right one, listen, ask questions, and then address the issue. But at the end of the conversation, make sure she knows that you love her and support her even if you disagree with her decision.

The bottom line is: Don't judge her. Love her. You can disapprove of what she does without disapproving of her. So love her through it all...good and bad. No matter what. Encouragement goes a long way with this generation...and to be honest, with *all* generations. We all like to be encouraged. We all like to be valued. So tell her when she's doing a good job. Tell her when you realize she is making great decisions. Tell her when you see her confronting issues and people in a different, a better way than she did a year ago. Tell her when you see changes happening in her life. How awesome to hear these things from someone who loves you and you love them back!

7. Pick your battles.

I have the picture in my head of a stack of poker chips. We keep collecting them as relationships progress and then there comes a day when you need to cash a few in. These are the days that you see some bad choices or an attitude that has crept up. This is the time to play your chips. You know the old song, "You got to know when to hold 'em, know when to fold 'em."

The same goes for mentoring relationships. There are times that you have to listen, hear, tell them what you've learned in your life and what God has taught you through similar circumstances. But then there is that yellow or even red flag waving frantically in the wind. These are the times where you play your relational chips.

You've earned the right to speak into her life. You're seeing warning signs or danger flags all around a situation. This is the time where you pray hard, suck it up, and lay down your hand. These moments are few and far between. But they are also times when God calls you to be him with skin on. Who will tell her what she needs to hear if you don't tell her?

Pick your battles wisely. If the battle is she wants a tattoo, that's not a hill to die on. But if she's thinking about moving in with her boyfriend or starting to get swept up into a bad crowd, that *is* a battlefield worth dying on. Don't mother her, or judge her. Tell her truth, but *always* in love!

8. Look for the God moments.

While you're on the journey with her, there will be all kinds of moments. Moments filled with fun, laughter, sadness, and tears. Be aware in the midst of the times when to add the God moments. These are the perfect times to interject something God has taught you in your life. An event or memory where God moved powerfully and taught you something. Even in the midst of disciplining your kids, she can see the way a Christian family should operate. And if you screw up in that area, you can talk to her about that too. There are God moments in every happening. We just need to be aware of them and ready to act on them.

9. Be the initiator.

"O God, you have taught me from my earliest childhood, and I constantly tell others about the wonderful things you do. Now that I am old and gray, do not abandon me, O God. Let me proclaim your power to this new generation, your mighty miracles to all who come after me."
Psalm 71:17-18

"Only the living can praise you as I do today. Each generation tells of your faithfulness to the next."
Isaiah 38:19

Throughout Scripture there are passages such as these where we are instructed to pass on what we know to the next generation. The Bible never says, "Wait until they come to you, then teach them"!

That's why this shift in thinking is so important. *We* need to be the ones who keep looking for those God puts in our path. *We* need to be aware of the God moments and act on them. *We* need to look through the lens of "I want to be your friend," not "I want to disciple you."

I've been looking through the Scriptures, and it's pretty rare to find a mentoring relationship that was initiated by the mentee. For the most part, the mentor is the initiator. Yes, there are exceptions, but when it comes to extended relationships, they were initiated by the person who had been around the block a few times.

Examples? Paul chose Timothy, Moses chose Joshua, Jesus chose his disciples (except for Andrew—and he was a referral!). The point is we need to change our lens and start initiating relationships with the younger generation.

⚶ 10. Keep your own walk fresh. ⚶

As you start on this journey, you'll realize that you will grow as much or more as the young woman God has put in your life. God will start teaching you things and start opening your eyes to different perspectives. You'll find the Word starts taking on a different perspective. You start reading it with her in mind. And how you can minister to her…and others God will put in your path in the future. So read, have quiet times, stay current, keep up with trends, but most importantly—stay in the Word daily! God will speak to you and through you!

This story has special meaning as Meagan is my daughter.

⚶ ⚶ ⚶ ⚶ ⚶

I adore my three boys, but sometimes I just need to hang out with a girl. Despite our age difference, Meagan and I have a lot in common. We both like chick flicks, creative things, Mexican food, and shopping. Our shared love of ice cream sealed the bond. She made my life more fun. I loved going with her to movies, out to eat, and shopping at Dead Betty's, that funky thrift shop. It was really fun!

Meagan has always been a bright spot in my life. My boys loved having her around, and she seemed to fit right in with our family. Whatever we were doing was fine with her. Whatever we were having for dinner was fine with her. I always liked that she never used the front door, but used the garage door, just like my family. She enjoys life, and her enthusiasm rubs off. Being around her has inspired me to get out of my comfort zone and jump into life.

I see in her a heart for people. She values others. She takes time out of her life to hang out. I have always felt whenever I see her that I am not interrupting her life, but that she is really glad to see me. That makes me feel special. She is approachable. People of all ages like her.

Meagan and I had the opportunity to go to Africa together. While we were there, we went into villages and immediately Meagan was surrounded by dozens of kids who wanted her attention. She started holding hands, holding kids, and interacting with everyone. She spent the trip showing God's love to people who desperately needed it. I loved sharing that amazing trip with her.

Connie, I have also watched you allow Meagan the freedom to make choices and allow her to be who she is. I have seen your relationship with her, how you have spent time with her and talked to her, and now I see you reflected in her passion for life. Because of you and Lance, Meagan has gained a confidence and assurance in the way she lives life. I want to give that to my kids. So I guess you were mentoring me!

It has been a joy to watch Meagan grow from a little girl who loved God, to a teen who was sorting things out, to an amazing young woman who has made her faith her own. It was so awesome to see God honored and celebrated in her wedding. God's hand is on her life.

Thanks so much for including me in your lives. It has meant more to me than you'll ever know. Even though you may consider me a "mentor" in Meagan's life, I feel like she's taught me much more than I've taught her.

Lindy Bridgers
Las Cruces, New Mexico

FYI...It's All About Her!

(For Your Information—ONLY!)

Don't take this with you and take notes—that would be bad!

※ ※ ※ ※ ※

Here's a list of things you may want to eventually find out about whomever God puts in your life so that you can get a better picture of who she is and how she became who she is. This will help you pray for her more specifically. It will also help you pray more clearly for wisdom for yourself in certain areas. But this happens with time and through relationship. This list is not, by any means, intended to be a fact sheet or to-do list. It's simply a helpful reference tool for you as you get to know the amazing young woman God has put into your life.

Name..

Age..

Brothers/Sisters ....

Mom/Dad ....

Where do they live?..

Are they married/separated/divorced/living?...

Is she single/married/separated/divorced? ....

Does she like to travel? Domestic? International? ....

....

Passion for___? ....

....

Schooling ....

Career ....

Hobbies ....

Success ....

Dreams for the future ....

....

What are her thoughts on marriage? ....

....

Morality Meter? ....

Currently involved in a relationship? ....

Recently involved in a relationship? ....

    What went wrong? ....

    What was right? ....

Animal lover? Pets? ....

Conservationist? ....

Vegetarian? Other special dietary things to remember? ....

....

Religious background? Did she grow up in the church? ....

....

Does she come from a Christian home? ....

What age did she start attending church? ....

With family? friend? by herself? ....

Currently attending church?...

Is she curious about spiritual growth?...

Is she currently in a small group or Bible study? What is she studying?

....

Other

....

....

....

....

....

....

....

....

....

....

....

....

....

....

....

....

It started with a girl doing cartwheels on the beach. She was young, new to gymnastics, and I was a coach. While helping the girl with her form at the beach retreat, I met her mother. Her mother was the wife of the pastor of the young generational ministry. She had been a hairstylist some time ago and offered to cut my hair anytime. I immediately took her up on it. Free haircut! Woo-hoo! That's how it all started. That's how she began to walk with me.

Susan actively became my mentor for the next six years. It didn't start off in a women's church meeting…with me, a young 20-something, longing for mentorship, leading, and guidance from an older, wiser woman in the Lord. I wasn't hoping and praying for the right match. It started with an older, wiser woman in the Lord looking out for the younger generation. She knew I needed mentoring, leading, and guidance simply because it was a biblical idea, and she was a Bible-following woman.

We began meeting on Tuesdays, informally. It worked with her family and my work schedule. I was fairly new in the area, an avid volunteer at church, and she was a woman with a heart for the next generation of women. Susan and I met at her house or the mall or at her daughters' volleyball or basketball games. We'd talk in the car en route to do errands or to go shopping for her latest house accessories. Sometimes we'd go to the bookstore to get the latest Christian book that she had read and thought would impact me. We'd do laundry together while her kids were doing homework upstairs and her husband was at the elder's meeting at church. We'd cook dinner together while her oldest daughter was watching TV and her youngest was practicing the piano for her lesson the next day. We'd go shopping at the outdoor outlets, of course, for the latest bargain or simply just to have a place to walk and talk. We'd meet for tea, coffee, lunch, dinner, or breakfast. I'd dog-sit when she needed it if I could, and I'd offer to take the girls to spend some fun time with them, to have another older woman in their lives to talk to, outside of their own mom. Susan trained me how to be a mentor as she lived it; she didn't need to teach me with words.

Susan was, and continues to be, a great mentor and role model. She would answer my phone calls of the latest drama, and sometimes chose to ignore the drama, knowing in her heart I needed to rely more on God than on her. She protected her family. When we were supposed to meet and something within her family revealed greater importance, we were postponed. Susan rarely gave her opinion. More often, she led me in asking questions leading back to God, teaching me self-learning with the Teacher himself. We talked about the books she recommended and always reviewed the truth of the Word within our daily lives for application. Susan listened, watched, and allowed me to join in her life.

She modeled what she taught. She never offered a book she didn't read herself. Never offered a Bible study she wasn't doing herself. Never offered advice she hadn't swallowed herself or advice that wasn't asked for. She gently reproved when necessary and lovingly never judged, even during confession of my sin. Like Jesus, she listened, and like the woman at the well, I left feeling love and forgiveness from someone who just found out everything that I had done against the Lord. Every single time I left her presence, I felt the joy of the Lord and the freedom of forgiveness.

Through Susan's modeling, I saw a Christian marriage. Not a perfect one, but a God-honoring one. I saw her and her husband out-serve each other. She didn't have to tell me about serving my one-day-

to-be-mate…she allowed me into her life, her home, and her family's life to learn and see for myself. She didn't try to be something she wasn't but offered me all she was. She shared the wisdom she had gained from her marriage, children, family, and own life experiences. She loved me where she was at. She loved me where I was at. She enveloped everything I have looked to in a mentor since our time together.

I have since become a mentor to many younger women in my life. Susan has since moved across the country, and I, soon to marry a missionary, will travel the world by boat and spread the news of Jesus Christ, Lord willing, worldwide. I now look for that younger woman. I listen. I pray. I keep my eyes open, my heart aware, and my mind in tune for the next woman that Jesus will place in my path. I encourage others, even teens, to be looking for the younger ones the Lord will place in their paths. And I implore the older generations to take the challenge and accept the responsibility to offer themselves to those younger women around them. You are needed. We need you. We need your love, life, example, lifestyle, and help. You don't need to be perfect. God has built you perfectly for us.

Since my time with Susan, I have mentored many, fallen in love with the younger generation, and sought out the older ones for the precious jewels of wisdom they have to offer. I have been blessed to build a young women's ministry where we can talk about women's issues and be biblically based women of God, in a non-fluff, reallife manner. I now am blessed with the opportunity to see Jesus' love lived out all over the world by traveling with my soon-to-be-husband and offering the same, everyday love and guidance that were once offered to me every Tuesday.

It doesn't take a seminary degree. It doesn't take a lifetime of struggles or a perfect marriage (of which I hear there are none ☺). It takes two women and willing hearts. God will guide the rest and change lives through it.

I owe Susan so much and all the other mentors since, who have willingly chosen to delve into my life and, in the end, have a part in making me the best woman for Christ I can be, no matter the circumstances. Thank you, Susan, and thanks to all of the other incredible women out there who give daily the talents they have to those of us who are thirsting to be just a regular part of your day. Thank you for your willing hearts. And thank you for your love.

Karyn Long Blanc
Metro Washington, D.C./NOVA

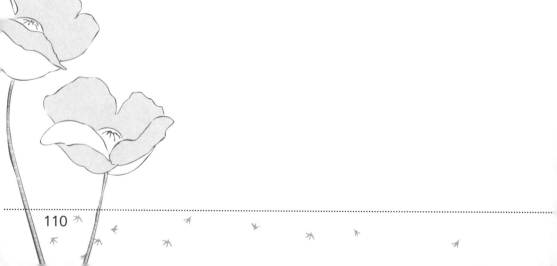

I Get It...
What Now?

Let's do a quick recap:

• Lifestyle mentoring is a matter of changing your lens to see the women God has already placed in your life (or very soon will!) and starting to develop a relationship with them more intentionally.

• There is no program. You simply invite her to join you as you walk through life together, be it at your home, running errands, or over coffee. Just do life together!

• Your curriculum is your life; your experiences, successes and failures, joys and sorrows; and most importantly, how God has impacted you through it all.

• Ignore the myths. There is nothing that Satan would like better than for you to believe the lies he's feeding you, or worse, just wait and don't do anything!

• Embrace the marks of mentoring. You could be doing this already! Just recognize it and act on it!

Now what...

Here are some steps for you to get started:

• **Pray** that God would start changing your lens. Pray that he would reveal young women in your life who would benefit from a deeper relationship with you. If you aren't aware of any young women in your life, pray that God would bring someone into your life and that he would give you the eyes to see her as he intended.

- **Start** developing existing relationships. Start changing your lens. Start inviting a young woman deeper into your life. Be the initiator. Start taking steps to begin building new and lasting relationships with the next generation. You won't be disappointed!

- **Develop** your life curriculum. Explore the sections we've provided where you can think about your own life and what you have to offer. Discover the times in your schedule that are mentoring opportunities in hiding and learn some good tips for connecting.

- **Connect** with a friend or two to partner with you in this journey. It always helps to have someone in your life, your age who's on the same page. Maybe you know someone who is already doing this and is just starting to realize it, or someone who is willing to jump in the boat with you!

Sometimes we can't see something that's right in front of us. It just takes a good friend to point it out. Ask your friends to be an extra set of lenses, on the lookout for a girl in your life who could benefit from a deeper relationship with you or a girl you could start being more intentional with. And encourage your friends to look for the young women in their own lives. Having a friend along for the journey can also be encouraging when you have minor snags in your mentoring relationship, as every relationship inevitably will.

"It's better to have a partner than go it alone. Share the work, share the wealth. And if one falls down, the other helps. But if there's no one to help, tough!"
Ecclesiastes 4:9-10, The Message

✻ A part of your women's ministry? ✻

You may want to introduce this concept of lifestyle mentoring in your church's women's ministry. Let me make this clear. This shouldn't be a *program* within itself. It should be a component of your already existing programs. Just take these principles, lay them out for your women, and then make it a point to do a weekly, biweekly, or monthly checkup.

For example, check in with other women who are mentoring to see if your lenses are being refocused. Are all of you seeing girls in your lives differently? Are your lenses still a little cloudy?

Have women who are mentoring suggest times when you could be more aware of your surroundings and whom God has put in your path. What are their names? What are your next steps?

Talk about what you are learning from the younger women. What are you learning about yourself through these relationships? How are you developing the relationships?

Are there prayer requests you can share with the group concerning the women you are mentoring (while maintaining confidentially of course)? Be sure and share praise reports! Tell those around you how God is working.

Share how God is keeping your walk fresh! Share how God is using you in someone else's life. Wow! How powerful!

Once lifestyle mentoring is introduced into the DNA of your women's ministry, the rest will fall into place. You will start viewing everything you do through the lifestyle-mentoring lens. It will become a part of you, not just an "add on" ministry or program. You won't need outreach programs because your lifestyle is all about outreach. Once you start implementing this into your life, everything and everyone around you changes. You will start seeing everything through the filter of impacting the next generation.

God has given you the opportunity to touch someone's life. You may see her clearly, or you may not see her at all...yet! But she is there. God has given *you* the story that she needs to hear and the tools to help her grow.

Jesus knew the benefit of spending time with people. He knew that the only way for his followers to see the authenticity, the reality of his deity was to watch his life. Through their relationship with him they were able to go out and tell others about him.

He wants you to do the same!

I like to sum this up with the picture of two women walking down the road of life together. Keep this picture in mind and use the word *WALK* to help you remember the key points of lifestyle mentoring:

W—Watch

Watch for those God puts in your path.

Change your lens.

A—Allow

Allow young women into your life.

Allow God to work through you.

L—Look

Look for the God moments.

How is God growing you and the woman in your life?

K—Keep

Keep it real! Be authentic.

Keep it fresh! Keep your walk with God fresh.

Walk through life with someone else...the two of you *together!*

You can do this!

Write It Down!

We invite you to take the following pages and write down what God is teaching you about

Yourself

Jot down the things God brings to mind about your own journey. The things God has taught you through your successes, failures, hurts, and joys. Go through the list provided. Pray, meditate, and really think about the journey God's brought you up to this point. Write down what big things he's taught you, how he taught you, and those God used to speak into your life during those times.

Look at the calendar. Write down opportunities to have someone come along with you. Start praying about the "who" in your life. Who has God put in your path that is a few steps behind you on the journey?

Her

Once you have recognized "her," write down how you met, the connection, the start of the journey, and the things you are praying for her about. Write down moments that you share together, insights she has that impact *you*! Fun times and memories are always great to remember. If there are concerns for her, write those down and pray, pray, pray! God will give you the perfect time to share those concerns with her.

Use the following pages as a prayer guide. Write specific things to pray about for those God puts in your life. What a great way to keep track of what God is doing in her life and yours!

"For the Lord is good. His unfailing love continues forever, and his faithfulness continues to each generation."

Psalm 100:5

"It is no use walking anywhere to preach unless our walking is our preaching."

—St. Francis of Assisi

"If you want to go fast, go alone. If you want to go far,
go together."

—African proverb

"We will not hide these truths from our children; we will tell the next generation about the glorious deeds of the Lord, about his power and his mighty wonders. For he issued his laws to Jacob; he gave his instructions to Israel. He commanded our ancestors to teach them to their children, so the next generation might know them—even the children not yet born—and they in turn will teach their own children. So each generation should set its hope anew on God, not forgetting his glorious miracles and obeying his commands."

Psalm 78:4-7

"Now that I am old and gray, do not abandon me, O God. Let me proclaim your power to this new generation, your mighty miracles to all who come after me."

Psalm 71:18

"Preach the Gospel at all times. If necessary, use words."

—St. Francis of Assisi

Recommended Reading

Group's Emergency Response Handbook for Women's Ministry
(Group Publishing, Inc.)

Ever find yourself at a loss for words when a friend shares about a difficult life situation? This book is packed with practical advice for when a friend is going through a life-altering situation, such as cancer, rape, or an eating disorder.

Blue Like Jazz: Nonreligious Thoughts on Christian Spirituality
by Donald Miller

In this narrative novel, Donald Miller rediscovers his faith in Jesus and the church. This is a great read for anyone wanting an inside look at the postmodern believer.

Dear Church: Letters from a Disillusioned Generation
by Sarah Cunningham

In 14 letters to the church, Sarah Cunningham outlines the biggest complaints and concerns of the next generation when it comes to church as we know it. Not without hope, this book provides an outlet for and insight into the next generation's thoughts and perspectives on the modern church of today.

unChristian: What a New Generation Really Thinks About Christianity...
and Why It Matters
by Dave Kinnaman and Gabe Lyons

What do young Americans really think about Christianity? What are their feelings on the controversial issues of the day? Dave Kinnaman, president of the Barna Institute, has the answer to these questions and why these questions and answers are significant to us as a church in the new millennium.

The Bridger Generation
by Thom S. Rainer

If you are interested in learning more about the bridger generation (born 1977-1994), this book details the defining terms of this group as well as how to reach it.

Acknowledgments

There are so many people I would like to say thank you to. So let's get started!

Thank you…

Jesus! For changing my lens in so many ways. Thank you for changing my passion, though it was hard and painful at the time. Your ways are great and your timing always perfect.

To my kids, Jonathan and Meagan, the lights of my life. Your lives, how you love Jesus, and how you serve him now is such an incredible joy to my soul. I couldn't be more proud of both of you. I love you so much!

To my kids' spouses, Ryanne and Mychal John. Thank you for loving my children. Thank you for loving Jesus, serving him faithfully, and keeping him central in your homes. I love you both as if you were my own.

To my mom and dad. Thank you for raising me in a Christian home and for making me go to church. Thank you for loving Jesus so deeply. And thanks for loving and supporting me no matter what! I will always be grateful and will never take for granted the great example and foundation you gave me. I love you.

To the family and friends who spurred me on and encouraged me to write this book. I seriously didn't think I had it in me, but you kept telling me I did. Thank you for your tenacious prodding. I couldn't have done it without you—really, I couldn't!

To Cathi, who was the inspiration for this book. God is using and will continue to use you in big ways! Thank you for believing we could do this, for using your amazing writing abilities for Christ, and for your eternal friendship. You will always have a special place in my heart.

To Group Publishing. Thank you for taking a chance on me! Your encouragement and support have been amazing through this process.

Thank you to my husband, Lance. You are, without a doubt, the best thing that ever happened to me. I am who I am today because of your love and influence in my life! You are my partner, my best friend, my confidante, my one and only true love. Your integrity, impeccable character, and love for our Savior is such an amazing testimony. You say what you live and live what you say. Your favorite passage is 1 Corinthians 16:13-14, "Be on your guard; stand firm in the faith; be men of courage; be strong. Do everything in love" (New International Version). Your life is the perfect picture of these verses. You are an amazing man and I am a better woman with you in my life. Wow, Babe! What a ride… together! I love you!

Connie

Thank you to Amy Nappa and to all of the wonderful people at Group for taking a chance on a couple of unknowns and embracing the message of *That Makes Two Of Us.*

To Doug Slaybaugh for affording me the opportunity to research this generation I find myself so intrigued by, and all of the churches, pastors, and worship leaders who graciously tolerated my incessant questioning.

To my house church family. Annie, Carrie, Chris, Josh, Loisa, and Zak, for supporting and praying for me during my St. Augustine adventure.

To Barnes & Noble, West Palm Beach, for providing me with inspiration and espresso.

With special thanks to Connie and Lance Witt, Bill Dogterom, Michelle Danaher, and my loving family for walking with me through life thus far. I have been so blessed by your wisdom, prayers, and encouragement. I can't wait to see what lies beyond the horizon with you.

Cathi